The Insatiable Quest for Beauty

A young woman's guide to overcoming our culture's obsession with perfection

By Tiffany Dawn

ISBN: 1475272553
ISBN-13: 978-1475272550

Some names have been changed to protect the privacy of certain individuals.

Edited by Susan Kenney
Cover design and photography by Amanda Robinson,
www.lovelikethisphotography.com
Cover design concept by Joshua Misla and Amanda Robinson, Rochester, NY
Book layout by Pauline Wegman and Tiffany Dawn, Rochester, NY
Illustrations by Diana Ohene, Rochester, NY
Girl in Mirror line drawing by Danielle Bowman, Binghamton, NY

Unless otherwise stated, all Bible references are taken from the NKJV:
Hayford, J. W. (Gen. Ed.). (1979, 1982, 1991).
Spirit Filled Life Bible: New King James Version.
Nashville: Thomas Nelson Publishers.

Drawing by Danielle Bowman, 2006
Used with permission

Dedicated to my mother:

Thank you for your patience and stability
during my quest for beauty,
and for showing me how to live as a woman of God.
I am so thankful to have you in my life
as a mentor, confidante, friend, and so much more.

~Prov. 31:28-31~

Acknowledgments:

I couldn't have done this alone. Over the six years I spent writing this book (and the ten years I've been dreaming it up), so many people have been involved. I want to pause for a few moments to thank some of them.

To my editor Sue Kenney – thank you for believing in this project and for your enthusiasm while editing the book. I hope we get to work together again in the future!

To my friend Kelly Hopson for doing pre-edits and proofreading on this manuscript – you are way too kind. Thank you for being willing to read through this book several times, point out the confusing parts, look for grammar errors, and make sure everything was ready to go to my editor. You are wonderful!

To the talented, creative people who made this book look fabulous: Amanda Robinson, Pauline Wegman, and Diana Ohene – I am so grateful.

Thank you to my incredible focus group (and friends): Jess Best, Deb Cline, Rachael Frank, Adrienne Meyer, Traci Morley, Kim Reinagel, Kay-Leigh Stacy, Krysta Stacy, and Moriah Wiesner. I am honored and blessed that you took the time to read through the chapters, meet regularly to discuss them, and give me your honest feedback. Without your insights, this book would not flow the way it does (particularly chapters three and four).

Thank you to Rosie Obi, MS, LCAT, MT-BC, and Staci Whitney, MSW, for reading through this book from the perspective of clinicians working with adolescents with eating disorders. I so appreciate your wisdom in pointing out the areas that could be triggering to some, and your encouragement in the process.

Thank you to my dear friends and family who have read through this and then given me feedback. I don't have room to name everyone, but I wanted to name a few: Kellie Leigh, Alyson Mullie, Joanna Pape, Joel Peers, Allan Robison, Amy Robison, Liyah Robison, and Cate Vivacqua. Thank you for your honest observations, perspective, and enthusiasm!

Thanks to Nate Cronk and Greg Best for believing in this project, speaking vision and truth into my life, and giving me the kick in the pants I needed to finally get this book out there! Thanks to Moriah Wiesner for reading this book over and over, giving valuable ideas and feedback, co-writing the workbook with me, and being my friend.

To Ashley, Joanna, Joel, Justin, Karyn, Kellie, Krysta, Melissa, Rick, Traci, the Waltersdorfs, and the Zawackis: Thank you for walking this journey with me. You each have played significant roles in my life at different parts of the journey, and I am deeply grateful. Thank you to my mentors Pastor Mark & Diane DuPré – I love you guys so much! Thank you for everything!

To my family: Dad, Mom, Liyah, Andrew, Isaac, and Amy – thank you for putting up with me while I was on my quest, and for always being there for me. I love you guys – and our crazy (or "perfect," in dad's eyes) family!

Lastly, but *most* importantly, thank You, Jesus. This book is for You. You planted the thought in my heart and then You brought it to its fullness. This journey I've written about – even the most difficult parts – has been beautiful and amazing, because I've shared it with You. I am humbled by Your grace and mercy. Thank You that I've never walked alone.

Table of Contents
Coffee Date Topics

To the reader:

Hi! My name is Tiffany. I'm probably not much older than you; I started writing this book when I was nineteen, and now I'm twenty-five. I'm excited you're about to read it because I think you'll relate with many of the things that I talk about. As a teenager, I felt trapped in the black hole of beauty and perfection – looking just right, weighing the right amount, being seen with the right people. I thought beauty would bring confidence, but instead it started to destroy my life through disordered eating, obsessive thoughts, and hating the way I looked. This is the intimate story of my journey from that place of brokenness to a place of wholeness. Today I am confident, and not because I'm drop-dead gorgeous (I'm not) or dating the right people (I'm single). I'm confident and loved while just *being me*.

If I had it my way, I would share this story over a series of coffee dates. Each week you and I would meet for an hour. I'd share my story, and then listen to yours. We'd laugh, we'd cry, we'd hug, we'd pray. I can't have it exactly my way, so instead I have called these chapters "coffee dates" and filled each one with raw honesty.

This is my journey – the mistakes, the victories, the questions. I'm going to talk plainly about some difficult subjects, so as you read this, please talk with a trusted adult and/or a counselor if there are painful things this book brings to light in your own heart. I'll also be talking about my faith, as that was central to the freedom I found. I know you may not share the same faith background as mine, and that's perfectly fine. I think within these pages we all can find some truth to break through our struggles. Check out the things that worked for me, see if they would work for you, and then come to your own conclusions. My hope is that this book will give you the tools and motivation you need to begin your unique journey into freedom.

One more thing before I let you start reading: There is a fabulous (if I do say so myself) website for this book full of extra resources to help you along your journey. The site url is www.theinsatiablequestforbeauty.com. There you'll find video coffee dates of me talking about each chapter and then interviewing my friends, so you can hear other women's stories. I've also included deleted scenes (portions of the book that were in the original version), suggested reading and music, a downloadable workbook containing reflection questions (co-written with my friend Moriah), and more! My recommendation would be to read one chapter at a time, think about it, check out the website for that chapter, and then meet with a group of girlfriends to talk about what you've learned. (You can even use the workbook for a small group book study.) That'll help you to get the most out of our time together.

Okay, that's all I had to tell you before you get started. So let me invite you to join me on this series of twelve coffee dates — just you and me, sitting across from each other with our chais or lattes or whatever you want, transported via the pages of this book.

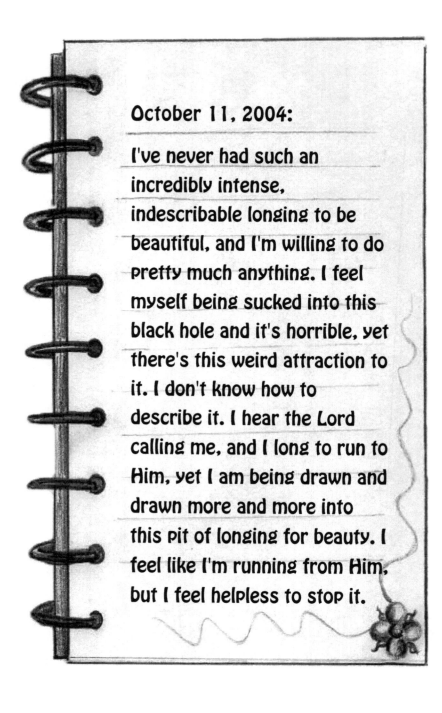

October 11, 2004:

I've never had such an incredibly intense, indescribable longing to be beautiful, and I'm willing to do pretty much anything. I feel myself being sucked into this black hole and it's horrible, yet there's this weird attraction to it. I don't know how to describe it. I hear the Lord calling me, and I long to run to Him, yet I am being drawn and drawn more and more into this pit of longing for beauty. I feel like I'm running from Him, but I feel helpless to stop it.

Coffee Date #1:

**I'm having a vanilla frappé - one of my favorites!
What are you having?**

To Be Beautiful

**"I check my look in the mirror.
I wanna change my clothes,
my hair, my face."**
~Bruce Springsteen, "Dancing in the Dark"[1]

The first notes of the bass guitar reverberated through the dark room. Fog billowed up around the musicians and played hide and seek with the colored stage lights. As it dispersed, I could see him: My gorgeous, talented boyfriend. Warmth lingered around my waist where his arm had rested moments before he had dashed onto the stage. He had winked at me then, making my heart skip a beat.

It was a full crowd that night and I almost felt like the "band chick." Seated on my traditional folding-chair-throne, I guarded the band's merchandise and chatted with the groupies. Last week my boyfriend had given me an "I'm with the band" keychain – and I was letting that dangle conspicuously from my fingers, as though it was a wedding band.

It was perfect. Until *she* appeared.

I wish I could call her Cruella de Vil and be done with it, but she was far worse than that. Her thin, hourglass figure moved into the crowded room easily and lightly, as the heads that turned her direction one by one looked like a toppling row of dominos. She could have been mistaken for Cinderella, because she walked with the graceful power of a princess rather than with the ludicrous strivings of an evil antagonist. I swear the very walls held their breath at the sight of her.

13

Her eyes confidently swept the room, secure in the power of her beauty. All over the room I saw the guys' arms, which had been wrapped around their girlfriends a few moments prior, suddenly loosen as they turned their heads worshipfully, as though paying homage to a goddess. Maybe it was only natural, but my own beloved boyfriend's eyes lingered over her too.

Sudden pain seared through my heart. Why did she have to come? I felt threatened by her beautiful presence, and the way she seemed a little *too* interested in my boyfriend made me sick.

I'd seen her before. She was one of the band groupies, and she had to know I was dating him…not that it mattered to her. Those perfect eyes full of beauty and power kept resting on his face, and then turning my way for a momentary inquisition. In her every glance my ears burned with the unspoken question, "Why is he with you? I'm so much prettier than you are…"

I could hardly take my eyes off of my boyfriend's face. When would he look back at me with his killer smile that let the butterflies loose in my stomach? When would he notice me? *Just look over and wink at me!* I wanted to scream. *Something – anything! Let her know you're with me!*

But of course he didn't look at me, not for more than a second anyway. When he did meet my eye, it didn't count. It was a quick, cursory glance that seemed to say I was just a tag-along, rather than the band chick. Dethroned, I crushed my "I'm with the band" keychain into my palm. Of course he didn't notice me. That kind of thing only happens in fairy tales, when you're the beautiful, powerful heroine, the one who causes even the walls to hold their breath.

How would it feel to be that heroine? I couldn't help wondering. *What I would give to spend a day – just one day – in someone else's shoes! Someone powerful and beautiful, who walks into a room and everyone notices. But then again, would I be able to give it up when the day was over?*

I snapped back to reality. Right here, right now, I was not the heroine; *she was.* And my boyfriend had become completely oblivious to my presence in the room. He was flirting with her, enjoying her sideways glances and boldly shy smiles.

Has a guy ever looked at me that way? I took a quick inventory of my life. *Not that I can remember. What am I doing wrong? I have to lose weight. I have to learn how to do my makeup. Look at her hair! I have to buy a straightener. I have to dress trendier and more seductively. I have to ask God to make me beautiful.*

Of course! How obvious. The answer had been staring me in the face all along. If I could be beautiful, my boyfriend wouldn't be able to take his eyes off of me. Cruella de Vil wouldn't be a distraction because he would be completely absorbed with me. *If I can be beautiful,* the thought suddenly came to me, *he will love me, and I will finally feel confident.*

The rest of the night was ruined. He didn't realize it because I hid it well, but the sinking feeling in my gut warned me that I might throw up. I should have expected it. This happened every weekend as he played his concerts. Not always the same girl, but always *the look.* The look and toss of the hair that said it all: "I'm prettier than you are. Why are you with him?"

I shouldn't have come.

Then again, he wanted me to be there to support him, and no way in heck was I going to leave him alone with those powerful beauties! I couldn't let them think he was available.

No, I had to be here. I just would have to hold in the pain and depression that washed over me. More than that, I had to accept and welcome these feelings. I had to find inspiration in them so that I could have the resolve to make myself beautiful, *no matter what the price.*

My eyes turned from my Savior. Having grown up with a strong Christian faith, never before had I stubbornly looked away from Jesus, toying with the idea that what society offered might be better than my relationship with Him. Sure these gnarly little thoughts had poked themselves into my mind many times over the years. I'd been dissatisfied with the way I looked, I'd counted calories, and I'd wished I were thinner, but it had never consumed me. Tonight was different. Suddenly I saw society offering a breathtaking, though unattainable, offer of beauty and I was captivated by it. I was determined to have it. I wouldn't let anything stop me.

My parents used to tell me that "inward beauty" was more important than my outward appearance. But now the thought came to me: *What have I gained from inward beauty? Nothing.* Because I had focused on inward beauty instead of outward beauty, I now felt threatened by *the look* I received from all those gorgeous girls at my boyfriend's concerts. My character didn't keep my boyfriend's attention. *No, inward beauty has not done anything for me.*

That night I left the concert on a quest for what I thought was true beauty: A pretty face with a perfect figure that turned heads. It was a quest to have the unhaveable, to attain the unattainable, and meanwhile I was captivated by a fleeting piece of vainglory.

the quest has begun

Thus began nights and days which turned into weeks which washed into months which vanished into two years of anguish: My insatiable quest for beauty.

I quickly dropped twenty-five pounds from a body that was not overweight to begin with. Surprisingly, the weight loss wasn't difficult. Every time I thought about those powerful, beautiful girls at his concerts, I lost my appetite completely. I never totally stopped eating; I just was so busy that the little bit I did muster up the stomach to eat wasn't enough.

It's hard to explain why I did this. I thought it was for my boyfriend, so he would notice me and not those other girls. But I have to admit it was also for those girls, so they would realize I *deserved* to be with him. Still my highest purpose was for myself — to gain confidence and security. I wanted to be that beautiful girl with the power that caused the world to hold its breath and make heads turn like toppling dominos.

I embraced the hunger just to be beautiful…and yet, looking back, I guess I wasn't as gorgeous as I thought. I was bony, stressed out, and losing clumps of hair as well as sleep.

I spent every waking moment consumed by my quest for beauty, and trying to rationalize its unexplainable thirst. Though I tried to keep up my reputation as a "good Christian girl," I stopped taking my faith so seriously. Beauty was everything to me, so I frantically shopped for the latest fashions, scarfed up articles on beauty tips, and counted calories. Some nights I cried myself to sleep, wondering if guys would ever notice me the way they noticed those girls at my boyfriend's concerts…and wondering if my dear boyfriend would rather be with a girl as pretty as that perfect blonde than with me.

Despite all the time and energy I poured into my quest, I still found that my efforts to become beautiful weren't working. What was I missing? That question haunted me every day.

what is an "insatiable quest"?

Insatiable.

When something is insatiable, it can never be satisfied. "Insatiable" is a longing that cannot and will never be completely filled. Chasing that thing is like chasing the horizon line; no matter how far you run, you will never quite catch it. Insatiable quests only leave you empty and broken.

Quest.

A quest is a Holy Grail, something you must have no matter what the price. A quest is a purpose that can drive you to the ends of the earth – if only you will find what you're after. It is your passion, your focus, where your thoughts and mind are constantly lingering – the one thing you want more than anything else. For some of us it's getting good grades, making lots of money, contributing to a humanitarian cause, or simply pleasing ourselves. Whatever is your driving purpose and motivation is your quest.

Beauty.

What is beauty? What was this powerful, elusive ideal that consumed me? The idea of beauty may be different for each of us, but for me it was being perfect, having it all together. It centered on weight and size – controlling the numbers on the scale and on the tag of my jeans. It was about my face, my hair, everything looking *just so*. Looking like the women I saw on television and in the magazines, like my boyfriend's ex, like someone I could never quite be. It was out of my reach.

no reason to stay

My boyfriend had a certain "look" he wanted me to have: Blowdried but not straightened hair; skirts or dresses; heels and white stockings (*weird, I know*). If I didn't look the way he wanted me to look, he would become upset and, sometimes, just leave.

One summer evening we went bowling with my relatives from Indiana. The heat made wearing stockings unbearable, and the idea of going to a bowling alley in a sundress made the hair on my neck stand up.

It was one of the few nights I actually felt good about myself; dressed in a striped American Eagle polo shirt (*he didn't like stripes or polos, mind you*) and jean shorts (*he didn't like jean material either*). I wasn't wearing white stockings, but that was okay because people didn't look at me as though I was from outer space. We saw some of the other guys from his band at the bowling alley and never had I felt more confident and attractive while talking with them.

As soon as we got back to my house, my boyfriend marched straight inside. He picked up his bags and walked back out the door.

"Where are you going?" I asked. "Don't you want to stay?"

"No thanks." He headed down the walkway toward his car.

I followed him, knowing something was wrong, and feeling a twinge of guilt at the outfit I was wearing. That was probably the problem.

He wouldn't talk to me as I hurried to keep up with him. "What's wrong?" I kept asking. "What did I do?" When he opened the door of his car, I panicked. "What's wrong?" I asked again, my voice straining.

He turned and looked at me. I will never forget his answer, as his eyes moved condescendingly, even disdainfully, from my head to my toes and back again. *"You're not giving me any reason to stay."* With that he stepped into the car, shut the door, and drove away.

I felt as though I had been punched in the stomach. Nausea overwhelmed me and the humidity of the evening suddenly felt closer and stickier than rain. It felt like a huge, clammy hand wrapped its fingers around me and started squeezing.

No reason to stay. No reason. No reason to stay. No reason. The words echoed in my mind and became both my mantra and my greatest, paralyzing fear. He had never said that to his other girlfriends. They had been able to keep his attention. Why? *Because,* I thought, *they were beautiful.*

Everything became crystal clear in that moment: If I didn't have it all together, I would never keep anyone's attention. I couldn't be myself. I had to become the "Tiffany" he wanted: the Stepford version of me.

i just want to be beautiful

I was crying again. I hadn't used to cry much, but lately I couldn't hold back the tears: Tears of self-pity, frustration, and of feeling insufficient and unlovely. Each night I laid my head on my damp pillow and begged God yet again to "please make me beautiful so that he will love me!"

One morning I was driving to school in a daze, as usual hardly remembering where I was or how I'd gotten as far as I had. That was when a song I had never heard before came on the radio and captured my attention from its first notes.

"...I count on the makeup to cover it all,
Crying myself to sleep 'cause I cannot keep their attention..."²

That was me. My mind flashed back: Night after night, head on my pillow, tears in my eyes. My greatest, paralyzing fear was summed up in that simple phrase: "I cannot keep their attention."

I remembered sharing that deep fear with my boyfriend. I was afraid to marry him because I had this sinking feeling that one day some other woman would capture him, body and soul. He only reaffirmed my fears. "It's like seeing a piece of chocolate cake sitting there and then telling yourself not to eat it," he said. "If I saw a beautiful girl who wanted to make out with me, I really hope I could say no, but I don't know for sure if I could."

Reading between the lines of the rest of our conversation, I felt that he extended to me a glimmer of hope, if you can call it hope: *If I was just good enough, it would work out.* That's how I always understood his actions and words. He expected perfection from me. Even though he thought I was lacking in outward beauty, he believed that if I had just enough inward beauty, I might be able to keep his heart captivated.

No. My hands slipped on the steering wheel. *I couldn't be good enough.* I never was, and never could be. I could not keep his attention.

"...Sometimes I wish I was someone other than me,
Fighting to make the mirror happy,
Trying to find whatever is missing..."²

How aptly put! Everyday of my life I wished I was someone other than me: Someone who could look in the mirror and see beauty looking back at her; someone like the beautiful, perfect girls at his concerts. What *was* missing? How could I fix it? Why didn't God make me beautiful?

"I want to be beautiful, make you stand in awe...
I want to hear you say, who I am is quite enough,
Just want to be worthy of love, and beautiful"
("Beautiful" by Bethany Dillon)[2]

I still remember exactly where I was at that stoplight turning onto Sunnyside Road. I could hardly see where I was going because the tears were pouring down my face as I cried out to God along with the mysterious singer. Somehow her simple lyrics had poignantly captured my heart's cry and my deepest desire. In that moment the brokenness of my heart surfaced.

My insatiable quest for beauty had begun. This desire for attention, or love, burned in me far more deeply than I'd known anything could. The quest consumed me. I was willing to give *anything* in order to grasp its unattainable breeze, which only lasts for a moment.

what about you?

I feel like I'm coming back from Memory Lane and reentering reality. I'm imagining that I'm sitting across from you in a coffee shop and slowly my eyes are refocusing on your face. Maybe there are tears in your eyes. (Or maybe you're about to laugh at my melodramatics.) But I hope that our hearts have connected for a moment. I hope you have been able to somehow see inside me through my vulnerability, and that you feel as though you know me a little better now. And I'm wondering: Can you relate? Have you ever felt that incomprehensible thirst for beauty? Have you ever wished you could be someone else, someone who seems to have it all together?

I want to invite you to come with me on eleven more coffee dates, so that I can share with you my journey. Though I have discovered that my quest for beauty will never satisfy me, I have simultaneously found the fulfillment of my desires. I have found Someone who satisfies me completely:

The One for whom I have searched my whole life, before I even knew what I was searching for.

Tiffany's Coffeehouse:

www.theinsatiablequestforbeauty.com

Check out the link to "1: Vanilla Frappé." Watch the video, where I interview some friends, all of whom have felt insecure at one time or another. It's amazing how even the women who seem to have it all together can still feel insecure. I've also linked in a YouTube video of Bethany Dillon's song "Beautiful" – see what you think!

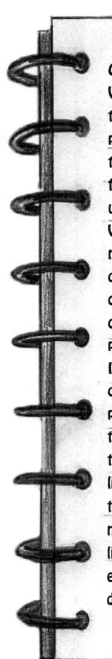

October 2, 2004:

Why did my boyfriend's ex-girlfriend have to be so beautiful? Why can't I be that pretty? I have lost my appetite so many times just this week—just today!—cuz I felt so sick to my stomach cuz of how unworthy and incomparable I am to her. Why can't I be beautiful like that? Why, no matter how much weight I lose, doesn't my waist appear much smaller cuz my hips shrink too? Why don't clothes fit right? I feel so inferior and not pretty enough to be with my boyfriend. It's such a horrible feeling!! And then days like this, all I want to do is get plastic surgery... I see the models, the thin, curvy women...why can't I look like them? If I eat less and lose weight it is like a goal to work towards...a challenge to attain... What I weigh now is far too much weight; but there is no limit for how little I can get to. Why does my boyfriend even encourage me in losing weight? Why doesn't someone try to stop me?

Coffee Date #2:

I'll have a caramel cappuccino today, because I love caramel!
...Or anything sweet for that matter.
What are you having?

Breaking Point

"You see, I'm the bravest girl
You will ever come to meet
Yet I shrink down to nothing
At the thought of someone
Really seeing me...
I don't wanna go on living
Being so afraid of showing
Someone else my imperfections...
I will bare it all, watch me unfold"
~Marié Digby, "Unfold"₁

Listening to sweet ballads reminds me of the beauty that comes out of brokenness. Have you ever wanted to be better so that you'd give someone a reason to stay? Maybe it was a boyfriend, a friend, or a parent...whoever it was, did they make you feel like if you were only better, they would have stuck around? Singer Marié Digby's voice tingles with the sweetness of cinnamon sugar, its beauty moving my soul to the memories of my own brokenness.

I thought my quest for beauty would lead me on a glamorous path of being noticed by guys and worthy of love. I thought beauty would give me the kind of confidence that would last, the kind of joy that would satisfy my heart. So I was stunned to discover that my quest for beauty broke me into pieces and dragged me along a path *away* from beauty instead of toward it. The road to perfection was nothing like I had imagined. It turned out to be – by far – the uglier path.

price chopper ending

We met for the last time in the Price Chopper grocery store parking lot.

"Do you want the afghan and scrapbook you made me?" the familiar voice in my phone was my boyfriend's — that is, my ex-boyfriend's. *"If you don't want them, I'm just going to burn them. It hurts too much to remember."*

I had broken up with him over the phone while he was on vacation. Each time I had tried to break up with him in person, I ended up caving, so I had to resort to a phone call. Looking back, it seems strange that one person could hold me so powerless. That was why I hesitated to arrange a meeting time. I didn't know if I could hold out my resolve when I saw his eyes again — those eyes that worked magic on my heart. But I couldn't let him burn the afghan and scrapbook; I had to hold onto those emblems of our relationship, as though they were a shrine.

His car was already idling in the far back corner of the lot when I turned in at the light. He opened his door, holding the afghan and scrapbook, which were stuffed into double-bagged grocery bags.

"Hi." The word felt too small. I took the bags and settled them in my backseat before turning toward him.

"I've changed." There were tears in his eyes as he held out a CD labeled "The Reason" in his fluid handwriting. "It's a mix of songs for you. Just listen to it." (I found out later the songs were supposed to make me change my mind and run back to him, but I didn't make it through the whole CD.)

"Can you stay for a minute?" he asked. His puppy dog eyes watched me edge into his car. "The things I said weren't all true. The truth is: You are a precious treasure and I will be jealous of the man who marries you."

"It has to be this way." I counted the specks of dirt in the foot mat. The memories came to me with each piece of dirt staining the carpet. The memory of humiliation when his hand covered my mouth to stop me from talking in front of our friends, and each time he told me he had a hard time loving me since his ex-girlfriend was a ten on the beauty scale and I just wasn't that attractive to him. I could slap myself for getting down on my knees in front of him when he explained why he thought a good Christian girlfriend should call him master and get down on her knees to apologize for arguing with him. I remembered taking a picture with a guy friend and him tearing the guy's head out of the picture in jealousy.

I knew he had never intended to hurt me; he had just thought he had to be honest about everything – honest to a fault – and he had some weird ideas about how relationships should work. He really was a nice guy...but that didn't erase what had been said. Nothing could erase it. I had to take my eyes off the specks of dirt. There were too many memories.

How could I explain? I had tried before, but he said my fault was greater than his because I hadn't forgiven and forgotten already. He didn't realize that forgiveness didn't always mean forgetting, or that I was daily fighting a thousand vicious thoughts that kept me from moving past those things.

Instead of trying to explain myself, I pulled a cassette out of my pocket. "I wrote a song for you. It's called 'Lullabye.'"

"I don't want it."

My eyes smarted. "Please take it."

"No, it'll hurt too much to hear."

"Fine." It was a whisper. "Basically the song says that God is my conductor and right now He's not conducting our love song. I can only play the music He's given me. Right now that's the music of singleness."

It was silent a few more seconds, as we soaked in the lemon water of our last moments together. I leaned toward the door handle.

"Wait," his voice was husky. "Can we kiss one last time?"

I paused. "I suppose that would be okay…"

Our lips met once, softly, then we both pulled away. He shook his head. There was too much sorrow in the kiss.

I glanced into the rearview mirror once as I drove out of the parking lot. My look back was a hidden farewell to the part of my heart which had suddenly gone missing, buried in his soul.

almost satisfied

That week was the calm before the storm, the numbness before the aftermath of pain. Then the hurricane descended on me, ripping to shreds everything I had believed in. Who was God? Who was I? What was my role in life? What was I supposed to do with this quest for beauty, which was intensifying every day? I had found identity and security in my boyfriend, and suddenly that was gone. In its place, a giant, booted foot was crushing my heart with the pressure to look good enough to hook another guy. If someone else would like me, it would prove that my beauty existed – or so I thought.

The months passed. I checked out the girls everywhere I went – in the magazines, on MySpace, in the malls – sizing up my competition. I compared myself with every woman I saw, leaving my heart strung thin with a deep awareness of my own inadequacies.

Despite my obsessed hopelessness with the way I looked, I still felt an intoxicating power in my weight loss. I felt a rush of success and *almost* satisfaction when nurses, pastors, family, and friends worried about my weight. I felt worthy of love and wished, "If only my ex-boyfriend could see me now. He would know what he missed." I felt like the models. I felt beautiful.

But not happy. Somehow the beauty wasn't enough, the way I had thought it would be. It's true that my self-esteem skyrocketed when I was hardly eating anything. It's true that I felt powerful when guys checked me out. But for some reason that feeling of power was devastating, and it drove me to find every little fault in my appearance and do anything I could to correct those insignificant details. I may have felt beautiful (as long as I kept up my two-hour, high-maintenance morning routine), but I never felt loved, treasured, and priceless, just as I am. At all times I kept on a mask of perfect makeup, hair, and clothes, even when I went to the gym. I wasn't *me*.

One day I went for a run with a friend in college without doing my hair or makeup. We took the back roads so we wouldn't see anyone. Go figure that some of our guy friends drove by during the few moments we had to cross the main road. They tried to say hi, but I pulled my hood over my head, pinched it closed to hide my face, and ran for dear life. I couldn't let them see who I really was, because that person wasn't perfect.

the breaking point

Throughout my personal hurricane, I could feel a restlessness stirring in my soul, which I thought must be God trying to communicate with me. It frightened me to sense the seriousness of His tone as He insisted I decide whether to follow Him or to follow my quest for beauty. Night after night, lying in bed, I felt the decision I had to make sprawled out on my chest like a fifty pound bag of sand.

I knew the right choice to make, the right "Sunday School answer." But honestly I wasn't ready to let go of my quest for beauty. I wasn't ready to choose Jesus. I knew what was right, I knew I had to stop following this quest, but I was unwilling to give up my obsession with beauty because I was afraid of losing any beauty I had gained.

When I transferred to a Christian college four hours away from my home, away from my ex-boyfriend and all the memories, I thought the quest would magically disappear. But it didn't disappear. Instead, I reached my breaking point. I didn't have a job. I didn't have my old friends. And to top it all off, I didn't have a boyfriend. I was broken and all alone – it was me, God (whoever He was), and my quest for beauty.

Food consumed my every thought as I gained fifteen pounds that first semester. I became self-absorbed, discouraged, and willing to try anything to lose weight.

One afternoon as I was climbing the stairs, having skimped on most meals that week, I suddenly was overwhelmed with dizziness and had to grab onto the railing. I couldn't see anything for a few seconds, as I held on for dear life and tried to breathe deeply. *I guess my blood sugar is low*, I thought. *Maybe I should eat something.*

That nausea became a regular visitor in my life. After a day or two of "sparkling headaches" (headaches that felt like they shot electricity through my brain and interfered with my thoughts and senses), the dizziness would once again appear unexpectedly, and the hunger pains would hit me with staggering force.

That was when I would lose control. I'd stuff my face with anything and everything I could find. It was the scariest feeling, as though I couldn't stop eating even though my brain was screaming at my body to put down the food. I couldn't tell when I was hungry anymore. I had never felt so powerless in all my life.

I just had to lose weight so I could have that image of perfection and so I could get guys' attention. But each time I ended up bingeing uncontrollably and gaining back any weight I had lost when I limited my food intake. It seemed hopeless. I couldn't for the life of me figure out what else I could do to lose weight.

…Well, that's not entirely true. I had one idea. It was something I never thought I would do, which may be why it stands out so starkly in my memory.

I will never forget the night I thought I had found the solution to my quest for beauty. Walking into the bathroom, leaning over the toilet, seeing the jeering reflection of someone — someone else, for it couldn't have been me — in the water below. It could have been a moment of self-realization and self-reflection, but for me it was blatant denial. Seeing myself reflected there from the toilet; too stunned to recognize my own face in the water below me, the synapses of my brain too cold to make the connection.

And then there was the failure and shame in my inability to actually make myself throw up. Each time I tried, nothing happened. Not only had I lowered myself to the point of trying to throw up, trying to do something I had hated and thought disgusting, but I also failed in actually doing what I had despised. I felt repulsed at myself, like the ultimate failure, vulnerable and filthy.

There was nothing else to do.

My breaking point had come. I could pursue beauty, but instead of bringing me to a glamorous, wonderful life, it would take me on a path uglier than I could imagine. Or I could fall on my knees...that is, if God would take me now. Either way, the decision would involve a breaking. My only hope was that if I broke while on my knees, one day I would be made whole again.

what about you?

Have you too felt this kind of desperation? Have you ever reached a breaking point in your life? What did you do? The amazing thing is that even in our brokenness, we are worth so much more than we realize. As I started to fall apart on my knees, and let go of my quest, I began to see more clearly...

Tiffany's Coffeehouse:

www.theinsatiablequestforbeauty.com

Check out the link to "2: Caramel Cappuccino," where I've interviewed my friend Brittany about her breaking point, and how from that place she found herself. You can also hear the song "Lullabye" that I wrote for my ex-boyfriend, and watch the YouTube lyrics video of my song "Mask," which perfectly relates to this time of my life.

Dec. 16, 2005:

I can't sleep! I'm tossing and turning – thinking about what I've become! I'm so frustrated...I feel so fake and so disappointed in myself. It's like I can't even relate to people...I'm too fake to relate to those around me. For the first time in my life, I'm hiding my heart from those closest to me. I'm afraid they'll see the fakeness, emptiness, longing, hypocrisy in me. I'm afraid they'll just criticize or point out my many faults. For the first time, I've struggled and not told a soul. Struggled because I experience depression because of the weight I've gained, and deep frustration with myself for feeling unable to control my eating. Struggled with actually putting into action the thought I've had so many times of trying to make myself throw up. Struggled with the feeling of fear and dirtiness as I bent over the toilet... Struggled with my ability to starve myself by day and yet when I grew tired at night, feeling completely helpless to not give into my hunger – and bingeing seemingly uncontrollably. No one knows! I mention that I feel fat and I get a chorus of voices saying I'm not and I just want someone to understand but instead I shut down 'cause I'm "so vain" and I can't let anyone see deeper into the recesses of my heart...to see that this consumes me and almost

every waking moment... I'm afraid to let anyone come too close to my heart 'cause I'm afraid they'll see the fakeness under my mask. I can't be real with people 'cause they yell at me for talking about the one thing most real to me. I don't want people to know I think about that. God I don't know what to do! I don't know how to overcome this vicious cycle!

Fakeness for Reality

Who have I become/Can you see in my heart/Or have I pushed you away again/Afraid you'll catch a glimpse/Of the me that I've become/If you catch a glimpse of my soul/Don't point at the fakeness/And tell me I'm wrong/I already know that/You tell me I'm vain and fake/Concerned only with outward appearance/Did you know it's frighteningly true/Has it ever occurred to you/How dreadful and real this fakeness is to me/I already know, I recognize the fakeness/I already know, it's more real than life to me/I already know, this fakeness is reality/When I catch a glimpse of my soul/Did you know it overwhelms me/I begin to hate who I've become/And when I look in my Savior's eyes/Do you know I can't see how He loves me/Why He holds His arms to the tree/But I love Him for it/And I'll give everything for Him/I'll give this fakeness for His reality

Coffee Date #3:
**I'm having a peach iced tea, because what else could be so refreshing?
What are you having?**

Come and Rescue Me

"So let go, jump in
Oh well, what you waiting for?
It's alright,
'cause there's beauty in the breakdown
So let go, just get in
Oh, it's so amazing here
It's alright,
'cause there's beauty in the breakdown"
~Frou Frou, "Let Go"₁

Strapping on my heels, I stood for a final, long stare in the mirror. I hated that mirror and what it told me, but somehow couldn't imagine life without it.

I had been staring into it for a couple hours already as I curled my hair, smothered on the makeup, and tried on outfit after outfit. My bathroom counter was littered with clothes by the time I settled on a pink, flowing shirt that hid the extra padding around my middle, paired with my favorite jeans (the ones that made my butt look bigger, hips wider, and legs thinner). I wore something pink everyday; it was a new identity I was building for myself now that I was away at college. I had tight, pink sweatpants for the gym, pink dress pants for church, and a lacey white and pink top for girls' nights out, complementing my new bleached blonde hair and tanned skin. No matter where I went, I had to look just right. Like today – it was 8:45am and the only place I had to go was class.

I walked back into my room, careful not to wake my roomie. Even in the dim light from the half-open door, I could see the magazine cutouts plastering my wall. Looking at them felt like entering a dream world: Wedding rings, women in beautiful wedding dresses, the best bridesmaid's dresses, the cutest couple pictures. *(I was a little obsessed.)* I stopped for a few moments to take them all in again, to imagine I was one of those beautiful women who could turn the heart of a guy and make him fall in love with her forever. For a few minutes before walking out into the real world, I let myself escape to that place in my daydreams where I was the heroine, where I was drop-dead gorgeous, where I turned the head of every guy who passed me. I tried to take those thoughts with me as I picked up my books and left for class. That mental escape numbed me from the pain of hating what I looked like, the stress of always trying to look perfect, the frustration with myself for my overpowering cycle of eating, and the fakeness that was engulfing me. On the outside, I may have looked like I had it all together, but underneath I was falling apart: empty, broken, and hating the shell of a person that I had become.

Have you ever felt like you were falling apart and desperately needing to be rescued? That morning as I walked to class, I didn't know where to look or what to do, but I was aching inside. Underneath my pretty-in-pink persona, I was desperate for someone to come and rescue me.

israel's insatiable quest

One of the morning classes I walked to in a haze of daydreams was Old Testament. Transferring to a Christian school, I had to make up Bible class credits. At first I thought that was dumb, since I'd grown up in a Christian home and my mom used to read the Bible to us (cover to cover) at the breakfast table. Go figure that the Bible classes ended up being my favorites.

My Old Testament professor was personable and funny. He even offered to give bonus points to anyone who read through the entire Old Testament during the semester. Being the definition of an overachiever, I took him up on the offer. I figured it out to be 12 chapters a day, and found myself absorbed in the gold nuggets of truth buried beneath the familiar stories. Each day I'd come home from classes, sit in my butterfly chair underneath the wedding pictures, and read for an hour.

One day toward the end of that semester I came upon Ezekiel chapter 16, and it stopped me in my tracks. It was like the story of my life…only in the Bible!

We've all heard legends and myths about women who were famous for their beauty. Well in this story a woman named Israel receives the gift of beauty. She first appears in the story as an abandoned and ugly child. No one noticed her and she was left on the side of the road to die. God saw her when she was invisible to everyone else, and He had compassion on her. He rescued her, gave her new clothes, and fed her food fit for royalty. When she had grown up, He made her become the most beautiful woman in the world by giving her His glory.

She had been trusting God ever since He rescued her, but when she became beautiful, she started to trust in the beauty instead of trusting the Giver of beauty. Israel began to flaunt her beauty by throwing her heart and body to every man she met. Instead of increasing her good looks, this lifestyle degraded and stole the beauty she had been given. She ended up in a vicious cycle; a quest that could not be satisfied. No matter how many men used her body and told her she was attractive, she still found her thirst to be "insatiable" (verse 28).

Throughout this whole time, God was still there, calling her to come back to Him, but she didn't. She fell more and more into a black hole of looking to beauty for confidence. By the end of the story, Israel had returned to a place of brokenness and ugliness, abandoned again on the side of the road just like when God had first found her. She had to let go of her quest for beauty because she was so used and degraded that no one wanted her anymore. As she let go of her quest, God rescued her once again. Out of His incredible love, He promised to pay the price for all the mistakes she had made during her pursuit of beauty.

I couldn't believe it! That was my life! The more I tried to be beautiful, chase boys, and have guys check me out, the more worthless and empty I felt. And here I was, just like Israel – broken, alone, and needing Him to come and rescue me too.

terrified

Each day that passed I became more aware that the same God from that story, wherever He was out in eternity, was awfully close to me. Though I couldn't hear Him, thanks to all the static on my end of the line, I felt His finger on my quest for beauty. It wouldn't budge. I knew He wanted me to let go…and I was terrified.

If I gave Him my pursuit of beauty, I was sure He wouldn't give me anything in return. I assumed He would just take my beauty away and let me be miserable, unnoticed, unloved, and lonely for the rest of my life – a thought which made me shudder.

I didn't know that the quest would end up destroying me. I didn't know it would leave me broken and abandoned. True, I could see things weren't going too well, and I could feel that I was beginning to suffocate, but I was scared of being rescued from the prison I knew like the back of my hand.

strength to let go

At the end of that first semester away at college, I was home for Christmas break and decided to go to church with my parents. I was, yet again, dressed in pink and half-asleep in the back row of chairs when one of our pastors read something that dropped a spark of life into my heart:

"...'How long will you falter between two opinions?
If the Lord is God, follow Him...'" (1 Kings 18:21)

I was instantly alert. It was like God had cut through all the static and spoken *directly to me.* From that point on, I wasn't listening to anything else being said by the pastors; all I could hear was His voice, those words, going around and around in my mind.

"You can't be in-between anymore. You can't serve two masters. It's Me or the quest for beauty. Which will you serve?"

It was a clear-cut call: all or nothing. God's approval or society's expectations – surrendering my quest or continuing my pursuit of beauty. My decision.

A response was stirring up from deep inside me before I even realized it, from a place I didn't know existed. It was bypassing all my *ifs, ands,* and *buts*; overriding all my logic and human reasoning. It was as if something somewhere inside of me said, *"Yes."* It was an answer that came from somewhere deeper than my mind and deeper than my heart, but at the same time came from every part of me. I knew my decision. *Lord, I know that You are God. I will follow You.*

There I was: A pretty girl wearing pink in the very back of the church – legs crossed, back straight, and completely composed on the outside. But my heart was on its knees. On the inside I was thoroughly broken and overcome by grace.

It was a moment when heaven touches earth, in which the God of glory, the Creator of the universe, reaches out and touches the heart of a child who has taken one faltering step toward Him. In that touch, He grants strength beyond all human understanding – only it's a different kind of strength. It's the strength of heaven, which enables the outwardly strong to be weak, the outwardly brave to surrender...yes, even the outwardly beautiful to let go of their obsession with beauty.

Moved by His strength, I offered Him my beauty. I gave Him my life. I placed in His hands what I considered to be my rights: what to wear, how to live, and my insatiable quest.

It was a moment of sweet surrender, when beauty comes from brokenness, when strength is found in weakness. In that moment I glimpsed the prize I would gain if I followed Him. Thousands of years ago God told one of His people, "I am...your exceedingly great reward" (Genesis 15:1). Now it felt as though He was saying that to me. Something deep in my soul told me that nothing in this world could ever compare to that reward.

The pastor read one more verse, the only other words I remember from that service:

"Whoever desires to come after Me, let him deny himself, and take up his cross, and follow Me. For whoever desires to save his life will lose it, but whoever loses his life for My sake and the gospel's will save it. For what will it profit a man if he gains the whole world, and loses his own soul? Or what will a man give in exchange for his soul?" (Mark 8:34-37)

I was left to wonder: When I reached the end of my life, would it matter whether or not I had been beautiful? Might I find that along my quest, I had lost my soul?

what about you?

Have you ever felt trapped or lost? Realized that you needed to be rescued, that you couldn't do it on your own anymore? Maybe you, too, felt like fakeness had become your reality, and you longed to be made whole and real.

It's a strange feeling to look back on my story, because it brings me back to those moments in time, to all the overwhelming feelings. It's amazing how He truly has rescued me; how alive and real and whole I feel today. But it all came from this place of realizing that I couldn't do it on my own, and reaching out for Someone greater than myself.

As I begin to tell this next part of my journey, I'd like to share with you the steps I took toward wholeness. You see, the climb toward freedom will be different for each of us; however, like two rock climbers scaling the same mountain, we might use some of the same footholds along the way. From here on out I'll share the footholds I found on my rocky climb toward freedom, in the hopes that they may bring you closer to freedom as well.

Foothold #1: Begin to let go of the quest for beauty.

The first foothold I found in the rocky mountainside, the first move toward freedom, was in surrender. As long as I was clutching my quest for beauty, I couldn't start climbing. Once I let go and opened my hands, I could grab onto the first handhold and start my journey.

I know you might not be ready yet to let go of your quest. It took me a long time before I was broken enough to risk it. But let me give you this challenge: Surrender your quest, whatever your quest may be. You could even pray what I prayed: "God, make me ready to let go."

When you are ready, all you have to do is say "Yes" to the Lord. It's a decision you make to stop looking to that quest for your joy, and instead look to the Lord. You then slowly learn how to live that way, letting go again and again and again every time you try to pick your quest back up...until one day you finally surrender for the last time. This first surrender doesn't always feel like a magic moment, but it will be the beginning of a new journey for you.

Until next time,
Tiffany Dawn

Tiffany's Coffeehouse:

www.theinsatiablequestforbeauty.com

Check out the link to "3: Peach Iced Tea." Today's feature du jour? My friend Aria sharing the story of her rescue! And a deleted scene: My quirky frog story. I also have a picture of my wedding magazine "wallpaper," so you can see for yourself just how obsessed I was. Lastly, if you have my CD ("This Is Who I Am"), check out the song "Dust," which corresponds with this portion of my journey.

June 25, 2005:

I have searched the Scriptures for some bit of life, but I have run from *You*. Your word seems a little safer, but I don't know *You*. I'm writing and praying this with tears streaming down my face yet again – seems like a daily occurrence. I'm afraid to come to You because I don't know You. And because I don't love you like I used to – I want to, but I don't, and I don't know how. And I am so very unworthy – I have utterly and miserably failed You – turning my back on all You were in me to walk after some stupid JERK of a guy!! And I hate who I've become in (the) aftermath of (my ex-boyfriend).

"You search the Scriptures, for in them you think you have eternal life; and these are they which testify of Me. But you are not willing to come to Me, that you may have life," John 5:39-40.

I just want to love You
I just want to know You
I have chased the wind
And am not worthy
Of Your presence
But I'm done running
And I just want to love You

Coffee Date #4:

Goodness gracious - there's nothing like the taste of white raspberry hot chocolate! That's what I'm having. What are you having?

Donut Holes

**"There's gotta be more to life
Than chasin' round every temporary high
Would you satisfy me?"**
~Stacie Orrico. "More to Life"[1]

I may have surrendered for the first of many times. I may have made up my mind to let go of my obsession with beauty, but that didn't mean everything magically got better. In fact, some parts of my life got worse before they got better. Have you ever had that happen? It's like riding a rollercoaster, and just when you get to the top, it drops and leaves your stomach behind. That's how I felt, especially on weekends.

I *hated* Saturday nights. It seemed like my whole hall was dead silent, because everyone was off with people who cared about them – out with friends, home with families, or visiting boyfriends. It was just me sitting there in my room all by myself, feeling so alone. Thinking, *what is left?* No one was there to be impressed by my pink sweatpants and perfect hair; no one was there *at all*. It was the kind of "aloneness" that suffocates you, that almost makes you hold your breath without realizing it. I hated those nights, mostly because I couldn't hide from myself anymore.

During the week it was easier to ignore everything churning inside me. I was so focused on what other people thought of me that I didn't have to think about what *I* thought of me. But when I was all alone, had finished my homework, and couldn't fall asleep at 7 pm, I had to face the things I was hiding from.

It was painful. In those moments, I couldn't cover my loneliness and self-loathing with daydreams. I couldn't ignore the fear of being single or fill my emptiness with bingeing. It was all right there, frighteningly real and alive, like aching turned into stabbing. In those moments, I remembered *everything*. The things my ex-boyfriend had said and the worthlessness I had felt. I used to be so sure of who I was in Christ, so sure that He was all I wanted, and now I didn't even know who He was. Everything was a mess. So I'd lie face down on the floor and bawl my eyes out, asking Him who He was, who I was, and asking Him to heal me and fix me. I was raw, broken, and *real*. I wasn't trying to be something I wasn't, or to conjure up a smile. I just *was* what I was. And that hurt.

Have you had those moments when it's easier to be fake than to be real? When you hate the way your hurt comes alive? Looking back, those awful Saturday nights were the moments that changed me, the moments when I faced the emptiness head on and allowed the healing to begin.

I don't know about you, but I hate feeling empty. Isn't that the worst feeling ever? I tried to fill my emptiness with looking right, catching guys' attention, and getting perfect grades. When all that failed, I tried to fill it with bingeing uncontrollably, as though I could fill a spiritual emptiness with physical food. None of that worked. It all fell right through, as if there was a hole in my heart.

It reminded me of a show called "The Donut Man" that I watched as a kid. The Donut Man had funny, curly red hair and kind of reminded me of Ronald McDonald. He sang lots of different songs, including one that said:

> *Life without Jesus is like a donut*
> *'Cause there's a hole in the middle of your heart* [2]

The Donut Man was right about one thing: I definitely had a hole in my heart, and the emptiness was suffocating me.

the crooked staircase

One Thursday afternoon, as I was dreading another weekend, I walked out of my piano pedagogy class and suddenly stopped. I stood frozen like a statue as my classmates filed around me.

I was standing in front of the music building's back staircase, which is infamous for being steep and crooked. Climbing it feels like climbing a mountain, and if you lose focus you might plummet headlong. The stairs looked just like my life: Crooked, steep, exhausting. Here I was out of breath. I was trying to fill the hole in my heart, and *nothing* was working.

Standing there, I prayed a prayer that changed my life. Honest to goodness. "Lord," I whispered, staring at the crooked stairway in front of me. "I've heard that You can satisfy my heart, but I don't know if I believe that."

The words tumbled out of my mouth, "I guess I've always thought that I had to be married, or in a relationship, or at least *prettier* before I could be satisfied. You know, something else had to change in my circumstances for me to really be happy. I haven't thought that You could just step into my life and make me happy." A deep breath before the clincher, "But if You can satisfy me…*would You?*"

I'm not sure how to describe that moment. It felt like something supernatural took hold of me, despite my cynicism – something warm and comforting, something joyful that threatened to force a true smile into my eyes. It took me over, and I felt it in my heart right away. I never expected to feel something so beautiful, but I did.

Scarcely missing a beat, my mind piped up: *This won't last long. Ten minutes max. Don't get used to it.* But my heart dared to believe, like one tiny spark of hope, that I had reached the end of my staircase. Maybe, just maybe, this peace wasn't going anywhere.

cars, gasoline, and God

C.S. Lewis was a philosopher, scholar, and author in the 1900s. In one of his books, Lewis said that God created our hearts specifically for a relationship with Himself. Lewis said that trying to fill our hearts with anything other than God Himself would be like trying to fill a car with something other than gasoline and expecting it to run.[3] Cars don't run without gasoline. You could try putting orange juice, coffee, or even ten Red Bulls in the tank, but you'd find that gasoline is the only thing that works.

In the same way, our hearts will not run correctly unless they have the proper fuel. I tried all sorts of fuel – dating, beauty, fashion, excellent grades, good humanitarian causes, and just plain old busyness – but none of those fuel sources left my heart feeling whole or deeply satisfied. It always felt like I was coming up short, as though something was still missing somewhere deep inside me. I was afraid to let myself be still and think, because then I would become tremendously aware of an *absence* – the absence of *whatever wasn't there.*

I don't want to live a half-empty life. *I don't want a hole in my heart.* The only theory I have found that works in my own life is that God created my heart to be completed in Him. Unless our hearts have the right fuel, our lives will always feel half-empty. The only fuel I have found that truly fills my heart is a relationship with God through Jesus Christ.

life-changing nights

Those Saturday nights changed my life. I still felt lonely, but somehow they became a little more bearable. Part of me almost looked forward to them. I didn't always feel warm and fuzzy, and I wasn't on some weird spiritual "high," but I knew that God was with me. I knew that He was filling the hole in my heart. So I started thinking of my dateless Saturday nights as my "date night with God." (*I know it sounds corny; don't judge me!*) I read books, bared my soul in songwriting, wrote in my journal like crazy, and just sat there with God. I let Him show me my emptiness and replace it with His fullness.

It took many broken nights on my face, but here I am, years later, and I have even more of that same joy and peace I started to feel in front of the crooked staircase. That honest prayer I prayed was the beginning of a journey that led me to where I am today, with the hole in my heart filled. Since then, every day of my life I discover more joy, peace, and *fullness* through knowing God.

what about you?

Have you ever felt like there was a hole in your heart? What have you found to fill it and give you that feeling of purpose in life?

At this point, the journey had only just begun for me. Reading back over my journals from the years 2003-2007 was interesting, because the pages told of the intense struggle in my soul. In one journal entry I would talk about how much God loved me and in the next entry I would talk about how much I hated myself. It was interesting to see how even as I was pursuing Him, I was only just beginning to find freedom. It definitely wasn't an overnight change that happened in front of the staircase; it was just the beginning. Continually coming before Him in my brokenness – *again and again* – made me whole. So here's the second foothold for you:

Foothold #2: Fill up on the fuel that will satisfy your heart.

My second foothold, following surrender, was to open my empty hands so they could be filled with something – or Someone – that would satisfy. That in itself was a time-consuming journey, as every foothold was, but slowly I began to find confidence and a new fullness in my heart by re-starting a fresh, personal relationship with Jesus.

We were created like donuts – with a God-shaped hole in our hearts. My challenge for you today is to ask Him to satisfy you. It's not like everything's going to change at once, or you'll always have happy feelings, or your life circumstances will be miraculously different. But day after day as you get to know Him more, you will grow to find inner peace and joy to face whatever comes your way.

Until next time,
Tiffany Dawn

Tiffany's Coffeehouse:

www.theinsatiablequestforbeauty.com

Check out the link to "4: White Raspberry Hot Chocolate."
Hear my friend Leah's journey into fullness of life from her
brokenness. Also look for a devotional from my mom about
how you actually start seeking God – because that can be
confusing. In addition to the other resources you can find
online, check out the song on my CD called "Empty Hands."

July 15, 2005:
Psalm 36:8-9, "They are abundantly satisfied with the fullness of Your house, and You give them drink from the river of Your pleasures. For with You is the fountain of life; in Your light we see light."

I just get this picture of His children gathered around His table, focused only on Him...completely satisfied in Him...at this higher level of complete satisfaction that I can never find in the world. And it makes me feel jealous of them.

Lord, I am Your daughter, and I could be sitting at that table, fully satisfied, but instead I'm eating with the dogs. (How does dog food possibly look delicious?) Then I hungrily look at the table and all I see are my siblings in Your family...eating and being ABUNDANTLY satisfied, and I wonder why I'm not that good. But if I looked at You, I'd see Your arms wide open, saying, "All who are thirsty, come and drink." "Come to Me all who are weary and heavy laden." "I will come in and dine with him."

I will come Lord. I don't understand why this dog food is so attractive. It's like masked as a cheesecake when it's not. And on Your table is the real stuff.

Coffee Date #5:

**I'm all over the hot apple cider today;
it practically turns the world into reds and greens!
What are you having?**

Unconditional Love

**"I fell to the Father's feet
His words washed all over me
And all the scars you made
Watch them fade away"**
~ZOEGirl, "Unbroken"₁

I was moping around the house. My dad had found out some of the things that had been going on behind the scenes with my boyfriend. Now I felt like I could never please my parents again.

My dad happened to walk into the living room, where I was aimlessly wandering – one minute sitting at the piano bench, the next, reading on the couch. "Tiffany, what's wrong?" he asked.

My eyes blurred with tears. "Dad, I feel like I have let you down so much that I can never make you proud of me again," I blurted out, blubbering over the words.

"Tiffany," he said, coming and taking me in his arms, "I love you because you're my daughter, and I'm proud of you because you're my daughter." His voice quavered, and I could tell he was trying hard not to cry. "Yes, you've made some stupid mistakes, but you're my daughter and *nothing will ever change that.*"

There's something about being loved for who we are that brings freedom. Instead of trying to prove we are good enough, unconditional love gives us rest and lets us simply *be.* When my dad said those words, I realized that God was saying the same thing to me: "Tiffany, you're My daughter, and nothing will ever change that fact. Just like you will always be your father's daughter, so you will always be My daughter. Your position is unchangeable, unconditional. I don't love you because you're good enough or have made all the right choices; I love you because you're My daughter. You have my love and I'm never going to leave you."

conditional versus unconditional

In our bleeding world, we haven't all had the chance to experience love like that. We don't all have dads who care for us, or families that stick by our sides no matter what. But God wants to show you His love for you – the love that you don't have to earn or buy; you just receive it – the love that simply *is* and will never change.

The love my boyfriend showed me was conditional. It was there if I looked right, dressed right, and kept it all together. But if I messed up, didn't look right, or wasn't good enough, it was gone. Keeping his love was like walking a tightrope, and I was constantly afraid of falling off. It was a guessing game of trying to anticipate what he wanted, trying to be good enough, and trying to be beautiful enough. In my mind, the quest for beauty was a method of earning love, of being good enough for love.

But the love God has for us is unconditional. Whether or not we ever choose to follow Him, His love will still be there waiting for us to accept it. I can promise you one thing in this life: God's love for you will never leave. It doesn't depend on you. It just *is*, even in spite of you. You can rest in that truth.

letter from daddy

Sheri Rose Shepherd wrote a beautiful book full of love letters based on Scripture, straight to our hearts from God. This book brought tears to my eyes. It is called My Princess: Love Letters from Your King. I'd like to share with you just a few sentences from the second letter in the book, entitled: "My Princess...You are my precious daughter"[2]:

> You are a daughter of the King, and not just any king. You are *My* daughter, and I am the God of all heaven and earth. *I'm delighted with you!* ...I formed your body. I fashioned your mind and soul. I know your personality... I see your heartaches and disappointments, and I love you passionately and patiently. ...although I am God – My arms are not too big to hold you, My beloved daughter.

> Love,

> Your King and your Daddy in heaven

fairytales turned reality

Last week I went to coffee with my friend Jenna. We studied abroad together in Australia, and ever since then we've had one of those friendships in which you can pick up after months apart, and it feels like nothing has changed.

We were sitting at a booth in Jitter's Café when she said, "Tiffany, I feel like my name should be changed to Israel!" Her face was glowing like she had fallen in love, even though she had recently broken up with her longtime boyfriend. "You know Zephaniah 3:17 where it talks about God dancing over, singing over, and rejoicing over the nation of Israel, His chosen people? Well that's me; I'm like Israel! God's up in heaven dancing when He thinks of me; He *delights* in me so much!"

I think Zephaniah 3:17 is one of the most beautiful verses in the Bible, so read it for yourself a couple times, soaking up the passionate love with which God wants to infuse you:

> *"The LORD your God is with you,*
> *he is mighty to save.*
> *He will take great delight in you,*
> *he will quiet you with his love,*
> *he will rejoice over you with singing."*
> *(NIV, 1984)* [3]

Jenna reminded me of a story my mom tells. When I was five, my mom says that I would walk around the house, randomly smiling up at the ceiling. When she asked what I was doing, I said matter-of-factly, "I'm smiling up at God because He's smiling at me."

Like Jenna, I rediscovered that confidence in God's love for me. God delights in me. He rejoices over me. Knowing His love makes the whole world turn into brilliant colors. Everywhere I go, I know His love and I know that I am a beloved daughter of the King. I can stand tall.

When we let Jesus bring us into a right relationship with God (see "Afterward"), we become His children. Now let me break this down for you: If you are a daughter of God, who is called the King above all kings, then you are a princess. Yes, you. A princess. Welcome to fairytales turned into reality.

When you become a daughter of the King and Father who loves you unconditionally, you don't have to prove you're worthy of His love. None of us are worthy of His love. So no matter what you've done or how much you may think you've messed things up, you are His daughter, and He loves you. This doesn't mean He approves or agrees with everything you've done, but even in your messiness He still loves you. Fully. Unconditionally.

You are precious. Sometimes it's hard to think of ourselves this way, but I need you to accept these words for a moment. When you were conceived, God was saying, "There's my daughter! I am so excited for her life!" You were not a mistake; He created you on purpose and knew the number of hairs on your head (Luke 12:7). And today, no matter what you've done or where you've been, God is still saying, "I love her so much! She is my treasure, my precious treasure. She is beloved." (See Psalm 17:8, Zechariah 2:8, Romans 9:25, Colossians 3:12, and 1 Peter 2:9.) Read that again, this time replacing "she" with your name. *You* are a treasure.

Maybe you're thinking, "But you don't know me. You have no idea what I've done." No, I don't…but God does. And it hasn't changed the way He feels about you. I promise. In fact, He is particularly drawn to broken people. If you are damaged, wounded, and broken, then I can't tell you how excited God is to heal, restore, and transform you into His princess!

I want you to get this. I used to feel unworthy of this love, or prideful if I accepted it. But believing we are beloved daughters of the king is not thinking too much of ourselves; it's the truth. God is enthralled with you. He delights in you and treasures you. He will never leave you. Every time you read the Bible or spend time praying with Him, His heart could burst because He so desires to spend time with you. When my sister Amy was five or six, she told me, "When I spend time with God, I just go in my room and listen to the birds sing." She got it! She had that innocent understanding of her heavenly Father's deep enjoyment in her, without feeling like she had to work hard enough to earn it.

If you only take one thing away from this book, I hope it would be a deep, personal revelation of how much God loves you, how much He likes you, and how happy you make Him. If there's one truth that sets us free, it's this, because knowing the love of God changes our entire lives.

wemmicks and crocheting

The more I rested in God's unconditional love, the more I was able to be myself. I had spent the past three years hiding behind masks of the perfect person, trying to force myself into a mold of the Tiffany-I-thought-was-wanted. Now I began to slowly gain confidence and learn how to live as me. Instead of trying to act and look a certain way, I learned how to just *be*.

Max Lucado, a popular author and speaker, wrote a children's book called <u>You Are Special</u>.[4] The story is about little wooden people (Wemmicks) who have no life; all they do all day long is go around sticking stars and dots on each other. They give stars to those with nice paint and cool abilities, but dots to those whose paint is peeling or who are clumsy. There's this one Wemmick named Puncinello who is covered with dot stickers.

Through the story, Puncinello discovers the secret to making the dots and stars lose their stickiness: trusting the love of the woodcarver. Puncinello has to trust that he was made on purpose, that he is not a mistake, and that his creator says he is special. As Puncinello begins to believe what his maker has to say about him, instead of what the other Wemmicks say, the dots begin to fall off, one by one.

God is our "woodcarver." In Psalm 139, David writes that God "knit" us together while we were in our mothers' wombs, creating us wonderfully. I love this verse, because I am a crochet fanatic. (Who else would crochet on the beach in Australia?) Knitting, like the crocheting I do, is a time-consuming, deliberate process. It is not a haphazard method of throwing something together. When I create an afghan, I specifically choose the colors and design I want, spend hours and hours making it just right, and when I am finished, I absolutely love how it turned out. In the same way, God spent months knitting you together in your mother's womb. He made you deliberately, on purpose, and He is crazily enamored with how you turned out. You are not a mistake, nor an accident that was randomly thrown together. You were created on purpose.

In the mid-1800s, a young girl would get on her knees each night and ask God to give her blue eyes. In the morning she would run to the mirror and disappointedly see brown eyes looking back at her. Little did she know that one day she would thank God for her eye color. Her name was Amy Carmichael.

Amy became a pioneer in missionary and humanitarian history. She blended in with the native people of India (who had brown eyes) by wearing a sari and dying her skin with dark coffee. With that guise, she was able to pass for an Indian...*because her eyes were brown.* Had they been blue, she would not have been able to sneak into the temples, where only native Indians were allowed, and rescue more than a thousand little girls from temple prostitution.[5]

It breaks my heart when I see women hiding their lovely, intriguing selves and trying to be someone else who seems to have it all together. Suddenly high schools look like clone factories and girls aren't living as the people they were created to be. The person you are is not a mistake. It's not a "flaw." It's a gift.

how much do you love me, God?

If you've never done this before, it might seem like a weird idea, but take a minute and ask God how much He loves you. This is something I did during my long Saturday nights on my face. I'd just ask Him, "How much do you love me?" Then I'd look for His answers throughout my day, allowing His love to fill the hole in my heart.

Here's what my heart aches for you to hear Him say: "I would give anything to have you near Me. I even sent My own Son to die for you and then rise again, so you can be My daughter. He's coming again one day for you, and He can hardly wait. I *love* you, My daughter, forever and ever. So come to Me. Question Me. Let Me speak the truth about who you are, how you have captured My heart, and how I delight in you. Let your heart rest in that truth. Fall asleep in My arms as I sing a lullaby over you. Your heart is spoken for. You are Mine and I will always fight for you, because I never walk out on My daughters. For *you* are the apple of My eye. Yes, *you* are My beloved princess-daughter. I love you."

Let your heart dare to believe that these words were written for you: You – yes, *you* – are beloved.

March 10, 2006: Just the way He paints the skies each morning and each evening...the way He conducts the serenade of the birds' sweet songs...the way He puts diamonds in the waters...I'm telling you, it's all like a beautiful love letter He's writing JUST to ME. Every way I turn my head, He's right there telling me, with a smile of delight, "I love you – you are so precious to Me, Tiffany." It causes my heart to jump and sing and laugh...makes me want to explode 'cause I just can't hold it in! It always has to bubble out of me...I have to smile, I have to whisper back to Him, "I love you too, Jesus." It's as though He's always right beside me, holding me, helping me, carrying me...ceaselessly! He watches over me when I sleep and walks with me throughout each day. He comforts me. Oh how He comforts me!

what about you?

Knowing the love of God changed my life. I couldn't believe that someone like me could be loved so wholly, so unconditionally. I felt like I didn't deserve it one bit, and yet there it was. (And I couldn't reject it, because turning it away would be like turning away food offered by an Italian mama – you just don't do it!)

The coolest part was that this love didn't leave me where I was. It not only gave me confidence to be exactly who God made me to be, but it also gave me courage to be transformed into the fullness of who He wanted me to become. His love gave me room to grow; I was no longer trapped in the Stepford version of me.

Have you discovered an unconditional love that sets you free to be who you are? A love that you know will never change? It took time, but slowly the reality and truth of this love began to set in, and it brought freedom with it. This was the next foothold along my climb:

Foothold #3: Receive God's unconditional love – just as you are.

My next step up the mountain was realizing how much God loves me. He loves me! He delights in me, rejoices in me, and enjoys spending time with me. He wants me to live as me, rather than miss my life by always wanting to be someone else.

You are not a mistake, and you are not an accident. You are a precious, dearly-loved woman, carefully and purposefully created just the way you are. You are a miracle. It can be hard to believe that, especially when we don't feel like we're good enough to be loved. If you ever start to wonder if God really loves you, read Romans 8. It talks about nothing being able to come between you and His love. We need to remember this regularly. Ask Him, "How much do you love me?" and then when you read the Bible or listen to music or take a walk outside, be looking for His answer. My friend Esther calls those little, everyday answers God's "Post-it Notes" for us. Keep your eye out for the next Post-it Note of His love for you.

Until next time,
Tiffany Dawn

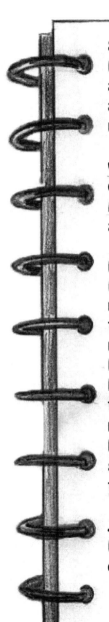

Sept. 16, 2005:

In the rain/All you tried to be/Is washed away/And when/The sun appears again/Who you truly are/Is all that remains/With no masks to hide behind

I am tortured with thoughts of my weight and looks literally every moment of every day...I feel like such a failure. Like when the day is over and I'm alone...what is there?

Dec. 8, 2005:

I am finding such joy and satisfaction in prayer...but I'm struggling with other things. Like...tonight I tried to make myself throw up because I hate the way I look. I determined that I really have to buckle down and not eat, since I haven't found myself being able to just eat in moderation. I just hate how I look. God's been helping me with that, but I still am struggling so much tonight. I don't want to look in the mirror tomorrow morning.

June 20, 2005:

I guess if I'm struggling it means I'm not dead yet.

Coffee Date #6:

I need some liquid courage for this topic,
so I'm getting a white café mocha.
What are you having?

Saying Goodbye

"I built a fortress with
a hundred thousand faces
I keep it safe with
a hundred thousand more
But these masks are wearing thin
As you draw me in"
~Starfield, "Shipwreck"₁

Thank God that I'm a hot mess.

Do you ever feel like a wreck? Like you keep fighting the same battles over and over? Sometimes I'm so intent on being "fixed" or "perfect" that I forget God said we are "earthen vessels," which by nature are easily shattered and broken (2 Corinthians 4:7). It's no surprise to Him that I'm a wreck, even if it surprises me. In fact, He chose to put the costly treasure of Himself inside of us. Earthen vessels are not safe places for treasure, yet that's where God chose to put the greatest treasure of all: Himself. Why? Because then when people see the treasure, they won't be distracted by its container or think the container makes the treasure more valuable; all glory will go straight to God.

Sometimes I'm so focused on getting it right every time that I forget that King David, who God called a man after His own heart, was a murderer and adulterer. I forget that Paul, who wrote basically half our New Testament, said he had not reached the goal and was far from perfect, but he was still going to keep pressing on toward Jesus. Paul also said that there were times when he did things he didn't want to do, instead of things he did want to do. Sometimes I forget that I'm *human*, and all humans have their struggles. The key is to keep pressing on, and every day to find more freedom than the day before.

This afternoon I told my friend Nate that I almost wanted my old eating patterns back, and I didn't know what was wrong with me because I hadn't wanted them in years. He said, "You don't have to be fixed. You're just as screwed up as anyone else. You know yourself and your tendencies, you have people you're honest with, and you know what you need to do to prevent yourself from falling back into this. It's okay; you're okay." I almost cried with relief, and when I walked out to my car I prayed, "Thank you God that I'm a hot mess."

i had to want something more

It was hard to say goodbye when the quest was all I could see, when it had become my very life. Have you ever felt that way? Have you had a situation when no matter how many people said you needed to let it go, you didn't fully listen until you'd realized the truth for yourself?

Take my ex-boyfriend, for example. My friends, pastors, and parents had told me I should break it off, and I tried to – time and again – but caved within hours every time. I believed him when he said he would change, that things would be different this time. Eventually my dad ended the relationship, but even then, I got back with my boyfriend a couple months later, and that time *I* had to be the one to end it once and for all. It was a long process full of many half-hearted goodbyes, but didn't end until I woke up and realized that I was better off without him, and that there was something else I wanted more than him (like my sanity, my relationship with God, and the dreams in my heart).

As many goodbyes as I said to my boyfriend, I said even more to my quest for beauty and disordered eating patterns. I say "disordered eating" because I was never diagnosed with an eating disorder. In fact, I don't remember the idea of an "eating disorder" ever crossing my mind. What did cross my mind was how frightening the whole experience was: how thoughts of food and weight consumed my life for several years, how I tried to eat as little as possible until I caved and ate everything, how I hated my reflection in the mirror. It's a scary thing to realize you're a slave to beauty, or to think you're in control of your eating habits only to realize they're in control of you.

One day in 2007 I journaled:

> I was trying to skip meals and eat nothing...and one day, in the midst of one of the sparkling, dizzy headaches I get when I haven't been eating enough, I was walking up the stairs and thought, "I wonder if I'm killing myself doing this." A little later I was like, "I hate this! I hate trying to eat nothing and then ravenously overeating as though I've gone insane and can't think clearly and then feeling tremendous guilt after and wishing I could throw up...and promising myself I'll do better at starving myself tomorrow! I'm so sick of this!"

That was when things slowly started to change, because for the first time I saw that I was better off without my disordered eating habits, and that I didn't want them anymore. Despite all the lofty (and unfulfilled) promises beauty made to me, once again I decided I would rather have sanity, my relationship with God, and the dreams in my heart. I couldn't have those *and* disordered eating. It was one or the other.

Where do you begin this conversation? It feels as though no voice is strong enough or gentle enough to capture the shame, the suffocating loneliness, the intoxicating power in weight loss, or the warm, strangling embrace of bingeing. Have you felt a gnawing feeling in the core of your being that you have lost control? That the mask has cracked and the weakness is threatening to spill over, but you just won't let it? I hope this coffee date gives you courage that you are not alone in the heat of the battle, that others have fought the same fight and overcome it, and that there is hope, even when things seem hopeless.

Many young women have asked me what I did to break out of my quest for beauty and its disordered eating cycles. My heart breaks when I hear their hopelessness, because I remember all too well the terror that this would never end, that it would consume the rest of my life. So let's talk about this journey to goodbye, this door to the rest of your life.

First let me clarify that I am not a counselor and this chapter is no substitute for seeking medical and professional help, nor would I ever begin to think this chapter has all the answers. However, these are a few things that helped me through my journey to saying goodbye for good – footholds that I hope will help you along your climb.

it takes time

As we talk about this door to goodbye, remember that it is a journey. You're finding your way, and that takes time. If you make a mistake or get tripped up, that's okay – journeys are full of potholes. We all fall down. The key is to stand back up over and over. If you were a toddler learning to walk, no one would get mad at you if you didn't walk perfectly on day one. Guess what – chances are you're not going to give up disordered eating patterns magically on day one either. It's going to be a process. But my friend Amy told me that she asks God to help her learn everything she can through her struggles, so someday she can help someone else through the same struggle. She said that if her battles miraculously disappeared, she wouldn't get to learn from them.

I wish I could say "enjoy the journey," but I know that's nearly impossible. So instead I'll say "learn all you can along the way," because along the journey you'll find yourself and the gift you have to bring to the world. Don't beat yourself up when you make a mistake; just get back up and keep going. It will be hard and the road will go up and down like a rollercoaster, but walking will become easier with time. (And with hard work.)

The first thing to do is talk about it. It's easy to put on a fake smile and hold it all inside. I thought no one would understand. It was hard to admit even to myself that I didn't have it all together. But when we hold our struggles inside, they have tremendous power over our lives. Somehow the simple act of sharing them with someone breaks a little bit of that power.

Instead of holding my obsession inside me, letting the thoughts swirl around like a dangerous whirlpool, I let it out. I have friends, mentors, and counselors I have talked with at different points in my life, because we were created to need other people. I meet with my pastor and his wife regularly, to work through many broken areas of my life. After one of our meetings I wrote: "As they were talking with me, I realized how false many of my assumptions and thought-patterns have been. You just don't realize it until you're confronted with truth." We can't usually see the truth on our own when we're trapped in disordered eating patterns, but someone on the outside can see and show us the truth.

As I met with my pastor and his wife, I started to see what issues were underlying my quest for beauty. Why was I so obsessed with beauty, weight, and food? There had to be a reason. Disordered eating can often replace our willingness to work through emotions in a healthy way. It can numb and distract us from the "real" (and painful) stuff of life. Instead of facing our fears, emotions, and lack of control in life, we continue in the cycle because it's easier to avoid the pain. However, until we really face those underlying issues, we will never be free of them.

I found that my disordered eating patterns were the result of the issue, not the main issue itself. For me, the eating habits came out of feeling unworthy of love and not good enough. If I didn't face those underlying issues and come to terms with the fact that I was lovable as an imperfect person, I would forever be trapped in disordered eating. As speaker Katy Hutchison said, you can't go around or over the pain, you have to walk through it.[2] I started looking at things in my past that had triggered my quest for beauty and the ways I thought about myself that caused it to continue.

Find a trusted adult, counselor, and/or a medical professional with whom you can talk honestly about what is going on inside your head. If you're not sure where to start, you could look up the "Eating Disorders Anonymous" website to find a support group that meets near you, talk to a school counselor, or find a youth leader at a local church to talk with. Let them help you. Like many things in life, disordered eating is just one area of brokenness that is too big to handle alone. That does not mean we are weak; it means we are strong enough to let someone else in to help us. (Note: If you think you may be struggling with an eating disorder, you should definitely talk with your doctor.)

Maybe you're reading this and thinking, "Well I don't struggle with disordered eating, but I do struggle with the quest for beauty or low self-esteem. Who can I talk with?" Find a trusted adult and/or a counselor. One counselor I met with pointed out that I was relying on feedback from other people to help me feel good about myself. She said, "Maybe you need to work on building a stronger internal sense of self-esteem, since what others say about you won't be a stable foundation." My counselor was able to talk with me about how to do this and give me resources on developing that inward sense of self-esteem. One book that helped me was Joyce Meyer's Approval Addiction. Youth leaders, school counselors, teachers, and parents are also wonderful resources. The important thing is to share your struggle with an adult you trust.

take control of your thoughts

When I was obsessed with my weight, all I thought about was food and the numbers on my scale. Now I have a different center for my thoughts. Instead of revolving my thoughts around how much I weigh, I think about things I am passionate about in life – things that *really* matter. I started asking myself, "What do I want my life to be remembered for – what I look like or the change I've made in the world around me?" Honestly, who gives a crap whether or not I was the skinniest or prettiest person? No one is going to remember me for that! Even if I was Miss America, people would forget my name. We have to focus on things that matter if we want to leave a legacy.

Finding a new center for your thoughts is easier said than done. It means recognizing the old, unhealthy thought patterns and kicking them out of your head. Some days that means that you will be wrestling with your thoughts from the minute you wake up to the minute you go to bed. I used to daydream myself to sleep at night with thoughts of what I would look like after a drastic weight loss. As strange as it may sound, those daydreams were hard for me to give up, because I didn't know how to go to sleep without them. I had to train myself to think of other things. One of the things I replaced those thoughts with was imagining I was speaking to young women about my quest, and what I would say. I've gotten some great inspiration for my seminar from those daydreams!

Joyce Meyer's book <u>Battlefield of the Mind</u> helped me learn how to stop the negative thoughts from running around in my head, and then to replace them with positive thoughts. It took concentrated energy and effort at first, and there were (and still are) times when I didn't win the wrestling match in my mind. That's okay! We won't win every match, so don't beat yourself up about it. Just get back up and try again. Every small victory adds up and gives you more strength for the next time. Eventually you will find that you hardly ever think the old, unhealthy thoughts, and when you do, you can kick them right out of your head.

find healthy coping skills

Find another outlet for your emotions, which I like to call healthy coping skills. Basically these are things you can do when you're feeling stressed or vulnerable. They are healthy ways to cope with difficult emotions.

Two of the emotions underneath my struggles were loneliness and fear of my imperfections. Instead of restricting or bingeing because of those emotions, I started to find healthy ways of coping with feeling that way. Some of my coping skills were writing in my journal, planning coffee dates with my friends, crocheting, and playing music. Writing songs became one of my main outlets. My friends tease me that most of my songs are sad and depressed-sounding...and they are. That's because they were an honest expression of my heart from moments of pain. They got those emotions out of me, instead of keeping them inside where they could tear me apart.

It takes time and practice to replace unhealthy coping skills (like disordered eating) with healthy coping skills (like songwriting was for me). Overcoming disordered eating (or an eating disorder) is not an easy or quick process; it takes hard work and time, but it's *worth it*. So find what coping skills are helpful for you. Some people feel blogging, art, being outside in nature, listening to music, or learning an instrument are helpful ways of coping. I have a much longer list of coping skills on my website, which you can check out to get some new ideas. The options are endless!

listening to your body

I didn't know what normal eating looked like, and I think many Americans don't know what it looks like either. Perhaps I was confused because of all the conflicting diet books and tips, but I seemed to think that normal, healthy eating was one of two extremes, and either I was going to become overweight from it, or I would always be hungry.

In reality, normal eating is a lot like grace. It's not a strict regimen to follow; rather, it's freedom. It's freedom to enjoy food and yet freedom from it taking over your life and controlling your thoughts and habits. It reminds me of what Paul wrote in the Bible (1 Corinthians 6:12 and 10:23) – that he is free to do as he pleases, but he doesn't let anything he does control him, and he chooses to do those things that are beneficial to him.

Likewise, we should enjoy the food we eat, but not let eating take over our thoughts and lives. Eating should not have the number one place of importance in our lives. We should make healthy choices (most of the time) regarding food choices and amounts, but also be able to enjoy what we are eating. Balance is key; everything in moderation. Listening to your body to know when you are hungry and what you are hungry for (mindful eating)[3] takes time to learn. Get to know yourself and find out what foods you truly enjoy.

When I was first overcoming my quest, sometimes I didn't "feel hungry," but my body would be able to tell me if I needed food. When I got headaches, was dizzy, or felt overtired, that was my body's way of saying, "*Please eat something!*" Make sure you talk with a doctor, nutritionist, and/or counselor as you learn what healthy eating looks like specifically for you.

know your triggers

As I shared with you earlier, my friend Nate told me, "You know yourself." That self-awareness helps keep me grounded. Knowing my "Achilles heel" (or area of weakness), allows me to be strong. If we are blind to our weaknesses, we are more likely to fall, but if we know our weaknesses, then we can learn what we need to do to be strong.

Here are two of my triggers: When I look at magazines full of beautiful, thin women and articles about how to change your life through the latest diet, I am tempted to revert back to my disordered eating habits. So I stay away from those magazines. I also used to spend too much time on Facebook looking at pictures my friends had posted. Inevitably I would end up comparing myself with them, feeling bad about myself, and starting to think about how to lose weight, so I don't "Facebook stalk" anymore.

When you notice things triggering you – or making you want the disordered eating – take note of those things. Then figure out what you can do to proactively avoid those triggers when possible, or how to handle them in a healthy way when they inevitably come. For example, when I start feeling triggered by something outside of my control, I set up a meeting with my pastor and his wife, a friend, or a counselor. It may be helpful to talk with a counselor or doctor as you get to know yourself and develop a plan of action that works for you.

faith

There has been some interesting research on the role of faith and spirituality in recovery from an eating disorder. The findings have suggested that having faith helps some people overcome their eating disorders.[4] I find this interesting, because faith played the biggest role of all in my journey.

As with the quest for beauty in general, you can't just give up one quest; you have to replace it with another. You can't just let go; you have to have something else to grab onto. My friend Joel compares it to being on a trapeze, or monkey bars – you don't let go of one handle until you grab hold of the next.

My faith was the rock under me, the handle to grab. I wrestled with it, re-explored it, questioned it, and ultimately found my healing in it. A song by Brooke Fraser says, "Everything I am for your kingdom's cause."[5] It's about giving every part of one's life for a cause bigger than oneself – namely for knowing Christ and making Him known. That is my greatest cause. It's greater than the way I look or the way I eat; it consumes me and gives me a purpose that is stronger than disordered eating. That, more than anything, showed me that my disordered eating was full of empty promises, but giving my life to something greater would give me purpose. Giving my life to Jesus slowly set me free as I lost myself in Him day by day and pursued Him with my whole heart. I wanted Him more than I wanted my disordered eating.

i said goodbye

Coming out of disordered eating is a journey. It's time-consuming, difficult, confusing, and has plenty of ups and downs. But it's *worth it,* because here's what you have to look forward to on the other side:

I no longer spend all my time worrying about what I'm going to eat for my next meal (or if I'm going to eat). In fact, I kind of forget about food. I don't try to forget about it so I don't have to eat it; I just eat when I'm hungry and then stop thinking about food until it's time to eat again. It's awesome! I feel so free! When I eat, I usually eat only until I'm full because the ice cream will still be there tomorrow and I don't *have* to eat it today, but sometimes I eat a little more because the ice cream just sounds so good right then. Either way, I don't feel guilty afterwards or promise to do better at starving myself the next day. In fact, I enjoy eating, and am able to eat in a balanced way, because *food doesn't control my life.*

I love who I am, what I look like, and being myself. I no longer wish I was someone else. I've made peace with the mirror and see myself the way I really look, not some distorted reflection. When I gain some weight (like before my period), it's okay because numbers do not determine my worth. On the other hand, I have reached a point in my recovery where I can work out on a regular basis without taking it overboard, since that's good for my health.

Does it all totally go away? Yes and no. I still have thoughts or temptations to restrict food – not nearly as often as I used to, but they pop into my mind from time to time. However, every day, month, and year that goes by, the thoughts become fewer and weaker. I think of it like an Achilles' heel – an area of weakness. Everyone has a weakness; mine just happens to be disordered eating. When we know our weakness, that self-awareness protects us, like Nate said.

Having thoughts come into my mind does not mean I've made a mistake. I just deliberately choose to get them out of my head. When the thoughts do come, I feel strong because my heart is full of God's love and acceptance, just as I am, and because I am in relationships with people who will support me and encourage me. The temptation to take up disordered eating habits is not wrong; the mistake is when we act on those temptations. The less I give into harmful eating habits, the less power they have over me.

Here's the other thing: Our feelings go up and down. That's normal. It's part of being a woman. The good news is: *You don't have to live by your feelings.* I realize now that I am loved no matter what I look like and no matter what I weigh. Because of that knowledge I enjoy every day of my life. Even on the days when I don't *feel* confident, I can *choose* to walk in confidence.

It all boils down to this: *I want something more than I want my quest for beauty.* That quest steals our lives, destroys our relationships, consumes our thoughts, and tries to spoon feed us the lie that we need it. However, life without disordered eating is free, satisfying, can leave a legacy, and leads to great adventures. I pray that you too can have an "aha moment" (as my friend Staci calls it) in which you realize what your quest really is and who *you* are – without the quest. Then, together we can close that door, say goodbye, and walk into the rest of our lives.

what about you?

Have you struggled with disordered eating, or not liking the way you looked? If so, what was that like? If you haven't started to do anything about it yet, what could you do? It can be hard to want to get better, and scary to start recovering. But you can do it! Disordered eating will never bring the wholeness it promises; instead, it destroys us. Take that first step or that hundredth step, wherever you may be along your journey, and you'll be one step closer to wholeness.

Foothold #4: Share your struggle with a trusted adult.

The first step to finding freedom from...well, from pretty much anything...is to share it with someone. Whatever your struggle may be, whether it's an obsession with beauty, feeling like you have to have a boyfriend to be confident (we'll talk about that more later), or an eating disorder, find a trusted adult to talk with. Just sharing the struggle with someone breaks some of its power over you, and letting them walk the journey with you helps you find freedom. If you struggle with an eating disorder, find a counselor and/or a medical professional to talk with as well, so they can help you say goodbye. You can also check out the National Eating Disorders Association website (www.nationaleatingdisorders.org) for more information, either for you or for a loved one.

Until next time,
Tiffany Dawn

Tiffany's Coffeehouse:

www.theinsatiablequestforbeauty.com

Check out the link to "6: White Café Mocha." My friend Rachel is going to share her recovery journey from anorexia. You'll definitely want to check this out and be encouraged! I also included a list of healthy coping skills; a handout about "normal eating" and what that can look like; and a list of awesome books, websites, and songs. Oh, and check out the song "Get Out of My Head" (on my CD). That's a great song for this chapter!

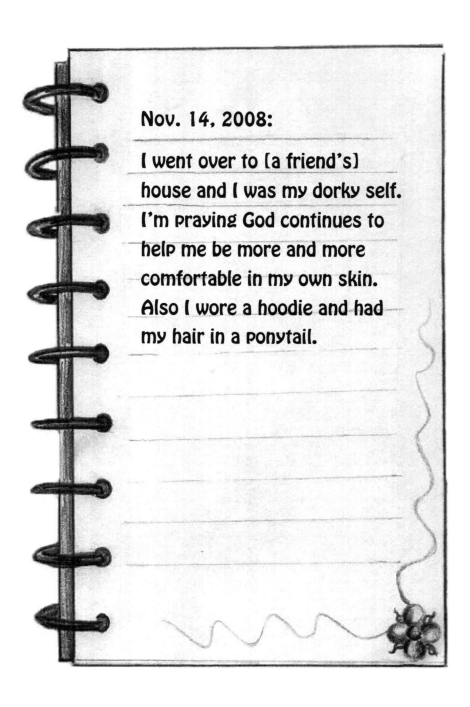

Nov. 14, 2008:

I went over to [a friend's] house and I was my dorky self. I'm praying God continues to help me be more and more comfortable in my own skin. Also I wore a hoodie and had my hair in a ponytail.

Coffee Date #7:

**I'm feeling adventurous today,
so I'm going to try a peanut butter frappé.
What are you having?**

A Healthy Balance

**"It is hard to find a woman,
especially a young woman,
in America today
who has a truly healthy
attitude toward her body."**
~Jean Kilbourne1

So is it wrong to take care of ourselves? Are we supposed to eat junk food all the time, stop working out, and wear garbage bags in order to feel happy?

When I first started speaking with young women about my journey, I thought it would be hypocritical to look nice. I seriously debated not washing my hair while wearing ragged jeans and no makeup to the first conference I spoke at, just to get my point across that beauty cannot be our confidence. Wouldn't that be showing girls that we didn't have to find confidence in beauty? Thankfully my mom intervened and said people wouldn't listen to me if it looked like I wasn't taking care of myself; they would wonder what else I wasn't taking care of. Good thing, as I probably would have begun and ended my speaking opportunities in the same day.

Over the past few years I've realized that I can care for myself without obsessing over or finding confidence in my weight or the way I look. I can have a higher confidence in God's love for me and still care for myself. Taking care of myself does not mean meeting a certain ideal weight or dressing a certain way; taking care of myself means developing certain habits that keep me healthy and enable my body to work effectively.

There is a big difference between obsession and health. When I was on my quest for beauty, I obsessed over the way I looked. I had to be a certain weight, always look my best, and I would put in as much time and effort as that required. Now I see girls who are on that quest, who put hours and hours a day into the way they look, and I don't want that anymore. Yes, I take care of myself through eating healthy foods (for the most part) and exercising regularly, but I am not going to put a third of every single day into looking my best. I have more important things to do – things that *really* matter and make a difference in the world around me. Now when I do not look my best, on those days when I've gained some weight or some acne, I can still feel confident in knowing that I am unconditionally loved. The way I look no longer determines my confidence.

So let me ask you: Are you being a good steward of your body, the body you have been given? A steward is one who cares for something entrusted to her, like housesitting. Are you doing a good job housesitting the body God gave you? Take a look at how you care for your body, talk with a trusted adult, and find the answer to that question.

Taking care of our bodies will look a little differently for each of us, but we all should take the initiative to ensure our bodies are working well, as that is our responsibility. Some ways we can care for ourselves are through getting enough sleep, eating foods that give us energy, taking time out of our busy schedule to relax (without feeling guilty), and so on. Maybe you like to dress up – go for it! I still enjoy dressing up and doing my makeup, and that's okay as long as it doesn't define me. At the same time, I am totally fine walking through the mall in sweatpants.

You see, many of these things I have been talking about, such as being thin or pretty or having the right clothes, are not wrong. It's not wrong to drive a nice car or to look beautiful; however, if we look to those things for confidence and joy, we will never be satisfied. My confidence is no longer based in what I look like; my confidence is in God's love for me. The important thing to remember is that caring for yourself is not about meeting a certain image or ideal; it's about enabling yourself to live life fully.

Let me put a little clarifier in here: If you have struggled with disordered eating, it is easy to continue in your obsession, claiming it is healthy. You should learn how to care for yourself healthily under the supervision of a medical professional. When I first walked past disordered eating, I had to keep a little bit of extra weight on for a few years. Whenever I started trying to get more toned, I ended up taking it overboard and going back into my binge-starve eating cycle. For me, keeping the lack of muscle for awhile was caring for my body. Again, don't do this alone. You can't see clearly when you're coming out of disordered eating, and you will need the support of trusted adults to learn how to care for yourself in a healthy way.

Let me share a few things I do to take care of myself, but feel free to take or leave the following tips. Find what works for you.

what works for me

#1: I buy outfits that fit.

When I was on my quest for beauty, I was all about the numbers. I was looking for the smallest sized pants that I could squeeze my hips into. Who cared if my "love handles" looked like a muffin top; I would feel terrible about myself if I went up a pant size!

Now I find clothes that fit me. The clothing size on the tag of my pants no longer defines my worth. (One of my friends actually cuts the tags out of her clothes, so she doesn't see the number. If that works for you, go for it!) I have also found certain styles that are more flattering than others, so I purposefully shop for those styles. I feel better about myself (and more comfortable) when I am wearing clothes that fit nicely, accentuating my shape without clinging to my body.

#2: I work out (doing workouts I enjoy) regularly.

I am not the kind of girl who loves working out or is naturally good at regular exercise. My roommate in college was extremely disciplined and loved working out. Not me.

Since college, I have started working out in a way that I enjoy. For example, I love taking walks, and could walk for hours. So I go on walks, either by myself to de-stress, or with my friends (it saves money too, since then you don't have to pay to go out to eat or to a movie). According to my mom and her research, at this time in my life it's really important to develop good bone density through strength training. So I joined a women's gym because they offer strengthening and conditioning classes that I enjoy.

Aerobic exercise? Mm, I pretty much hate it. I still force myself to do it semi-regularly since it's good for me. (*Note:* Obviously I am not *over*-exercising by any stretch of the imagination.) But for the most part I try lots of new things and then stick with the workouts I enjoy. Like an occasional kickboxing class – it's a great, cardio-blowing way to get my frustration out at the end of a tedious day.

Note: Working out can be a great way to take care of yourself – when you are able and cleared by a doctor. If you are struggling with an eating disorder, you may need to take some time without exercising in order to truly care for your body. Learning how to exercise in a healthy way should be done under the supervision of a medical professional. Talk with your doctor about this.

#3: I weigh myself less frequently.

I used to weigh myself all day long. Every chance I got, I'd step on the scale. If the numbers went up, I'd kick myself and know I had to eat less at the next meal. If the numbers went down, I'd feel awesome and inspired to see how low I could get. (Looking back, I now realize that was silly, since water weight changes throughout the day.)

Now I weigh myself almost every day, but only once. Although that's a huge improvement for me, this is still something I'm working on because ultimately I feel that I should weigh myself much less frequently. When I weigh myself every day, it automatically refocuses my mind on my weight. Lately I've been convinced not to step on the scale more than once a week. Our weight fluctuates throughout the day and throughout the week, and I don't think weight is always a good indicator of how healthy we are. My friends tell me they find clothes that fit them well when they are at a healthy weight (as determined by a doctor!), and then instead of weighing themselves they just notice how their clothes fit. I'm still getting there, but the less frequently I weigh myself, the less focused I am on weight rather than on health.

#4: I eat more slowly, filling up on healthier foods.

One way in which I ensured I was eating healthier portion sizes was to eat more slowly. Apparently it takes my body awhile to register that I have eaten something, and so I could eat nonstop for an hour and not feel full, but then it would hit me all at once and I would know I had eaten way too much. When I eat more slowly and enjoy my food, I feel satisfied, both mentally and physically.

While I am eating, I choose to enjoy my food. Sometimes that means doing nothing else, and just focusing on eating. Instead of feeling guilty for every calorie, I enjoy my meals. I've learned to listen to my body, and I try to eat what my body is telling me it needs…even when that means I need ice cream because it sounds just too good to pass up. (Can you tell I love my ice cream?) I can still enjoy the dessert without feeling guilty or planning to starve myself the next day.

As a matter of fact, I have one meal that I eat when I need to refocus and slow down. In order to remind myself to live in the here and now, I make tomato soup, put macaroni in it, and sprinkle mozzarella cheese on top. Then I eat it…very, very slowly, savoring every bite and paying attention to every sound, smell, and sight around me. When I'm done with my twenty minute, delicious meal, I feel refocused and as if life is no longer running away from me.

I also started looking into what foods were healthy. Once again, according to my mom's research, "healthy" does not mean the same thing as "low-calorie" means; healthy means food that is full of nutrients and energy to carry us through our day. I realized I ate so many carbohydrates and so little protein or fiber that I always felt hungry because nothing I ate stuck with me through the day. Adding fiber, whole grains, and protein into my diet gave me more energy and allowed me to actually feel full after eating.

Remember, everyone has a different body type and different needs. Talk with your doctor or a nutritionist and find out what healthy, mindful eating[2] looks like for you.

#5: Taking care of yourself could include dressing up or it could not. You don't have to fit a certain image. But if it does include dressing up, make sure your makeup isn't the basis for your confidence.

Not everyone enjoys dressing up. My sister Liyah would much rather wear sweatpants and a sweatshirt, and she can't understand how someone like me can spend three hours getting ready for a date. Her question is: "But…what do you *do* for three hours??" Well, that's just me. I love to dress up, and that's okay because it is not the basis for my confidence. I am still confident in who I am when I am not dressed up, and I no longer have to spend at least 1.5 hours a morning putting on a made-over image of perfection in order to feel good about myself.

I figured out that the hour and a half (or more) I used to spend in front of the mirror every morning added up to roughly 547.5 hours of my life in the year 2005 alone. And I thought I didn't have enough time to read the Bible! That is 547.5 hours that I could have been using my time more wisely and seeing eternal outcomes. There are still days when I spend an hour and a half primping – but for the most part I have now pared down that time in front of the mirror to a half hour.

In fact, there was a time when I had my confidence in the way I looked, and I felt like God asked me to give up my makeup until further notice. *He can't mean that,* I thought. But He did. So I gave it up for that period of time to remind myself that my makeup doesn't determine my worth.

If you like getting dressed up, then go for it! Enjoy that. I love being girlie and taking tons of time on my makeup before a date or a girls' night out. That's totally fine. But don't let the way you look define you or become your basis for confidence, because it will not be a stable foundation. Be a person who can dress up or dress down, because you are still the same person as a beloved daughter of the King, no matter what you are wearing. The way you look can and will change, both from day to day and over the course of your life. Make sure your confidence is in God's love for you, and out of that confidence, be free to enjoy dressing up or going to the mall in sweatpants.

what about you?

How do you take care of your body? What are the things that work for you?

Here's the essential difference I want you to see: It is healthy to take care of our bodies; it is not healthy to define ourselves by the way we look. Wanting to look beautiful is normal, but looking for our identity in beauty is where we go wrong. I want you to be free to live life as *you*. Whether you are dressed up or dressed down does not change who *you* are, and it does not change the fact that you are still loved. Take care of yourself. But keep your confidence in God.

Foothold #5: Take care of yourself, while keeping your confidence in God.

Be free to enjoy dressing up or going to the mall in sweatpants. Realize that who you are does not change based on what you look like. Jesus never judged someone based on outward appearance. Also realize that your body is His, and it is good to take care of ourselves so that we have the strength and endurance to do whatever He asks us to do. Whatever that means for you – whether it's eating healthier, gaining weight, exercising regularly, or trying to go to the mall without makeup on, take the next step toward caring for your body while keeping your confidence in God.

Until next time,
Tiffany Dawn

Tiffany's Coffeehouse:

www.theinsatiablequestforbeauty.com

Check out the link to "7: Peanut Butter Frappé."
I interviewed my best friend's mother-in-law, who is a dietician as well as a professor at my alma mater!
Hear her wisdom, from a dietician's perspective, about taking care of ourselves. In addition, check out the other resources online. (I don't have a song off my CD that specifically relates with today's topic ...maybe someday I'll write one!)

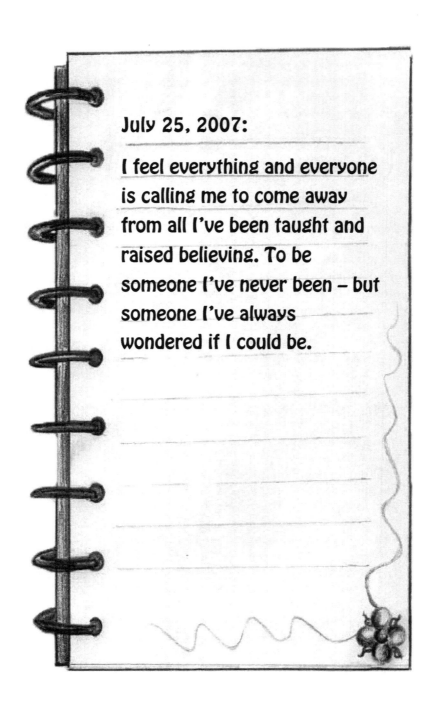

July 25, 2007:

I feel everything and everyone is calling me to come away from all I've been taught and raised believing. To be someone I've never been – but someone I've always wondered if I could be.

Coffee Date #8:

I'm thinking about the caramel macchiato today. It'll get me fired up!
What are you having?

Models, Image, and What You Can Do

"It must be hard to be a model, because you'd
want to be like the photograph of you,
and you can't ever look that way."
~Andy Warhol[1]

"I think you really have a shot at winning." His face was sincere as he watched me study the ad.

"Dan, c'mere!" a voice called across the quickly filling club.

"Coming!" With a quick wave to the newest arrival, he turned back to me. "Just think about it." Then he headed toward the bar.

Think about it I would! I was riveted by the bold poster with the caption "MISS INDIE." If I won this local heat, I would move on to the pageant in Brisbane. It seemed strange that I, an international student, was allowed to compete in this Australian beauty pageant. Then again, Dan knew everyone and could pull strings.

Me. In a beauty pageant. I could just die.

For years I had salivated over Miss America letters sent to my home, and earlier that year I had been accepted to compete in our local division. However, I had withdrawn so I could study abroad for my last semester of college. It was a hard decision, but I felt like I had to get away from everything and everyone I knew (which I don't recommend), so that I could try out the lifestyle I saw in the movies – dating lots of cute boys, going dancing with the girls, and maybe even modeling.

Studying the girls in the poster, I wondered what it would be like to walk down a runway set up right here in the middle of this club and have people judge me. Could I really win?

I'd made up my mind before I realized it. A few days later I maneuvered the public transportation system to the mall, where I would have my trial spray-on tan session. I'd been wanting to check out the spray-on tans for a long time, but I had always felt guilty spending money on something so frivolous. Yet there I was, and for the first time in my life, my ivory stomach was bronze.

Now for the real question: What to wear? There was that royal blue string bikini I picked up while touring the Gold Coast. That should bring out my tan. Or maybe the flowery, thicker bikini with the straps that crossed in the back, the one I bought specifically for Australia (because at home I didn't wear bikinis). Could I get away with a tankini? I'd always felt insecure about my stomach, although its new bronze hue gave an illusion of tone.

My old binge-starve cycle swallowed me back up like quicksand, though I hadn't needed to worry about my weight. I ended up coming down with the flu, followed by an allergic reaction to my medication. In other words, I lost too much weight, too fast.

The week before it was my turn, I headed down to the club to watch one of my friends compete in the first heat. I looked eclectic and classy in my sequined, silver shirt-dress with leggings and my hair looped behind each ear. I leaned into my usual spot by Nick, who was already so drunk he had dropped and shattered his beer glass. He snaked his arm around me.

"She's had some work done," I heard one guy saying of a girl with a perfect figure standing close by to watch. Two guys were keeping her company. "That chest and butt aren't real."

"But they look good," another guy said, ogling the contours of her body.

Was it possible to feel confident in a place like this? That girl with the work done seemed to feel sure of herself, but I didn't! Even with Nick here beside me I saw every flaw with myself and all the perfection in the competition.

Lights dimmed, a heavy techno beat began, and guys groped to find a spot where they could drool over the contestants. Here they came…

Outfit number one: Girl after girl pranced down the runway, trying to look sexy. Some bent over the judges to blow them kisses. The guys hooted, practically drooling into their beer glasses. The more hoots, the hotter the girl, apparently.

Outfit number two: One of my friends started her catwalk across the stage and I was horrified to hear a few boos. Kudos to her: she kept her brave face on and jutted her chin a little higher.

Outfit number three: The bikini. Here is what the guys had been waiting for all night. I could tell because they leaned a little farther forward, bent in clusters to make rude comments to their buddies, and hollered as loud as they could for the thin, tall girls. But for my friend, they only had boos and loud, rude remarks about her not being good-looking enough. I thought I saw a hint of tears in her eyes. I know I would have lost it.

What was I thinking? I was planning to put my body on a stage in the middle of a club? In front of a bunch of guys and girls and judges critiquing my every flaw, harping on my insecurities, and finding new issues for me to worry about? My stomach took a dive. I wonder if any of the other contestants were thinking the same thing.

"You'll do awesome next week," Nick whispered clumsily into my ear. He was too drunk to know any differently.

What was I even doing here? Why did I think this kind of life would bring confidence? Who the heck was I kidding? I would never look like a model, never compare with the magazine pictures. All these girls were looking for the fame and popularity that came from that supposedly glamorous lifestyle. They were looking for the power of beauty. But maybe its power was also its poison, driving one to pursue an unreachable perfection. Maybe our idea of beauty was so perfect it wasn't even human.

That lifestyle wasn't anything I thought it was. I didn't want to put myself up there and be judged like that. I had to get out of this. *Now!* I squirmed my way through the guys, trying to hide myself so they wouldn't judge me like they had judged my friend, to find Dan and tell him I had to withdraw from the pageant.

alone?

Back when I started out on my quest for beauty, I thought I was alone. I honestly believed that I was the only person who felt the way I did, and I was ashamed to admit my deepest, ugliest feelings to anyone. One day I journaled:

I cannot begin to describe the burning passion in my heart to be beautiful. I want to be beautiful inside too...but outward beauty seems so very attractive – like it's crying out tauntingly to me and each time I try to reach out and grab it, it completely eludes my reach. I SO wish I could describe the burden this is to me...the burning fire locked up within me and eating away at me and consuming me. These intense, insatiable cravings that are destroying me, and yet I somehow have a morbid enjoyment of it...this sickness in my stomach, perhaps birthed in jealousy and covetousness...*of all this I dare not tell anyone, or even write it all here...*for in this light it seems so ugly...

I didn't realize that I was surrounded by women facing the same insatiable craving, the same burning fire, the same haunting question as I was: "What am I missing?"

When I walked through the mall, literally feeling yellow with self-disgust, I was clueless that many of those women who looked powerful and beautiful to me were also feeling yellow. They were grasping at the same elusive beauty for which my hands were outstretched.

What I didn't know until after my quest for beauty is that four out of five women don't like the person they see in the mirror[2] while more than half may be seeing a distorted image of themselves in the reflection.[3] Eighty-one percent of ten-year-olds fear becoming overweight,[4] which most likely means they are already aware of society's expectations, such as the idea that being overweight is not desirable. The models we try to look like "are thinner than 98% of American women"[4]...and we are all affected. Looking at pictures of models in magazines – even for only three minutes – has a negative impact on women of all different ages, shapes, and sizes, according to a University of Missouri-Columbia study.[5]

What I didn't know is that the quest for beauty which I thought was unique to me had become a silent epidemic. I was only one of the fifty to seventy percent of American girls at a normal, healthy weight who somehow thought she was overweight.[6] I was only one of millions.

Jean Kilbourne, author, speaker, and activist, said that the media and advertising cause us to prize incredibly thin bodies and think that looking overly thin is normal. She says that even though a fashion model is thinner than the majority of the population and a "genetic freak," it is the majority of people (not the model) who are made to "feel abnormal."[7] Then we go and spend our money on products that promise to give us this desirable beauty. In 2008, Gordon Patzer, Director of the Appearance Research Institute, said people around the world spent 160 billion dollars a year on trying to make themselves more attractive.[8] Researchers have concluded that media plays an "essential role" in women's obsession with thinness, and that struggling with body image issues has become a normal part of life for young women in this media-saturated Western world.[9]

After I began to talk about my quest, women began to share their stories with me. One woman summed it up powerfully. She had been told her whole life she would be prettier if she were thinner. After losing seventy pounds and having liposuction, she said, "I can assure you wholeheartedly that body image…impacts your self image. I…still feel fat and ugly 99% of the time and it is coming from within me not from those around me."

I was not alone. This quest for beauty has swept away myriads of wonderful, lovely, strong women. Yes, even those women we look at and covet because of their beauty. They are being carried along in its tide, overwhelmed with guilt; trapped, ashamed, and silent. Many of them believe, as I did, that they are alone in the current.

my first box of teeth whitening strips

Her teeth glistening, she prances through the crowded restaurant as though it were a Hollywood ballroom, one long, waxed leg in front of the other. Every head turns toward her as she passes, and some jaws fall open. She can get any guy she fancies. Her secret? *Teeth whitening strips.*

Seeing these kinds of television commercials and advertisements all the time had me convinced this was why I was single: My teeth were too yellow! Honestly, do we really need teeth whitening strips? I mean were people dying or (even worse!) never finding a date before they were invented? No. We don't need them. But if advertisers can make us believe that we need them, then we'll spend money on them.

Why do we think we need teeth whitening strips? Because most of us want to be the girl who people notice, who can get any guy she wants. Coincidentally, that's the girl in the teeth whitening commercial, so of course we draw the conclusion advertisers want us to draw: We have to have teeth whitening strips to be that girl!

I used to beg God for the opportunity to spend one day as a girl who made every head turn. If whitening strips would do that for me, then I'd buy them! I remember walking through the aisles of a pharmacy/convenience store, looking for my first box of whitening strips. As I was comparing prices on the different brands, an elderly gentleman stopped and said, "You don't need those, you already have beautiful teeth!"

His observation stopped me in my tracks. My teeth were yellower than the models, and I had assumed that was part of the reason I was still single. But in reality, I was just buying into a marketing campaign to get me to spend my money on a product I didn't need. I'm not saying advertisers are evil. They're just doing their job – and doing it well. But we have to realize that they are selling us more than a product; they are also selling us an image of perfection. Why? Because if we can never look as perfect as their advertisements, then we'll keep buying their products that promise to make us look perfect.

what do models really look like?

Our culture is image-driven. We are each pursuing an image of some sort, whether through dating the right people, looking attractive, or driving the right car. Those things aren't necessarily wrong, but they will never satisfy us. We will always be looking for the next best thing to come along, but never reaching the perfection we want. Why? Because the perfection isn't even real.

The models we see in the magazines oftentimes don't look like the real humans who modeled for the photo shoot. The pictures are airbrushed and digitally enhanced to make the thighs thinner, the stomachs flatter, and the skin smoother. Sometimes shading is added on the stomachs to give the impression that the model has well-defined ab muscles, even when she really doesn't. Other times magazines have shown the face of one model over the body of another. (Even Julia Roberts has had someone else's body shown with her head on it!)[10] One girl asked me, "Why don't they just find a model who has it all?" As far as I can tell, that's because even models don't have it all; they are real people too! Our standards of beauty are so perfect that not even the models can live up to it.

Audrey D. Brashich wrote that a certain photo retoucher from New York City photoshops the ads for Cover Girl and big magazines. Brashich says that he claims that "for $20,000 he'll create a flawless cover image – no matter what the original looked like."[11] This means that the pictures you see in the magazines aren't what the models really look like, because not even the models look good enough for our standard of beauty. It means thousands of dollars worth of editing has been done to make those models look like they do in the advertisement. I have heard that actresses and models have said, "When I wake up in the morning, not even *I* look like the picture of me from that magazine." Heck, if that's true, you and I could be models if we had $20,000!

My brother Andrew does some photography for a friend of his who has started a Latin Vintage clothing line. After showing me pictures of his friend's website, with gorgeous models showing off the original designs, Andrew said, "Those pictures don't even look like the girls in real life. It's just about getting the right lighting. It's all about the picture."

And yet we think *we* have to look like those magazine pictures, when not even the models (who we learned are in two percent of the population as far as height and weight are concerned[4]) honestly look like that? Good grief! No wonder we resort to cosmetic surgery. No wonder *I* resorted to spray-on tans and teeth whitening strips!

Our entire culture has become perfection-driven. The people we are seeing are not real people. They're all made up to look perfect, *when people are not perfect.*

what are you gonna do about it?

Audrey D. Brashich wrote:

The truth is lots of girls *hate* trying to live up to "the look." They don't hate the idea of beauty or pretty things, just the feeling that they'll never look as good as the women considered beautiful – and the implication that they're less desirable, lovable, and valuable than those who are.

Everyone wants to be considered pretty…it's hard *not* to want it given the rewards and special treatment showered on those who are. But here's the truth: It's not our bodies that need changing or that need to look more like what's pictured most frequently in the media. It's made-up unrealistic beauty standards – promoted by companies that want to sell us products – that need to change to look more like us.[11]

So what are you going to do about it?

what are you talking about?

When I was in college, my girlfriends and I spent all our time worrying about weight and talking about our successes and failures with dieting. I hate to admit I tended to be the ring leader of initiating these conversations. Toward the end of our first semester, one of the girls blurted out, "Guys, am I fat?"

We stared at her like she had three heads. "No!! How could you think that?"

"Well, you guys talk about how you feel fat all the time, so I started to think maybe I should feel that way too."

Her statement shook me to the core. Was that the kind of influence I was having on my friends – making them feel badly about themselves?

A couple years later I was critiquing myself in a friend's room, when all of a sudden she stopped me mid-sentence. "Tiffany, when you're so hard on yourself, it makes me wonder how you see me. I think you're really pretty, and when you criticize yourself, it makes me feel like I must look awful."

Truth was, I hadn't thought twice about how she looked besides the fact I thought she was pretty, because I was too caught up in how I looked. Though I thought my negativity toward my body was only affecting myself, that conversation showed me it was also affecting others. I wonder how many times we say something negative about ourselves, thinking no one else is hurt by it, without realizing that even critiquing ourselves can cause others to feel insecure.

Ask yourself, "*How do I talk about myself?*" During my first year living away at college, I never once heard my RA (Resident Assistant) Kelly say a negative thing about herself. She wasn't proud either; she just didn't focus on herself, instead she focused on others. When she did talk about herself, she had an honest, healthy self image. *That's how I want to be!*

candy and biases

What we say is so important, because it can affect others even if we don't realize it. I mean, just think about it: My quest started mostly because of the things my ex-boyfriend said to me. He never meant to hurt me, but I was torn apart by the things he said without thinking them through. How often do we say something without thinking twice? Our words are *powerful* and can lift up – *or devastate* – others. Take a few minutes to explore your own biases and the things you say without thinking.

Here's one example: My friend Krysta gave me some candy in my Christmas present this year. As I was eating half the bag that night I said, "Krysta, are you trying to make me fat?" Then I thought, "Why would I say something like that, as though being fat would be a bad thing?"

Jean Kilbourne says that out of all the things we make fun of others for, being overweight is one of the only things that is still socially acceptable to be prejudiced against. She calls "weightism" our "last 'socially acceptable' prejudice."[12] Why? If I gained weight, would I have less worth? If I lost weight would I have more worth? *No*, but the things we say sure seem to suggest that!

Explore your attitudes toward weight and beauty, even subconsciously. For example, do you compliment only people who are thin, or do you compliment everyone? Do you compliment people who are losing weight, and if so, why? Do you choose friends based on who's popular or cute enough to be in your circle, or based on similar interests and values? On the other hand, do you avoid people or assume they're shallow, just because they're pretty? Look for the true things that give people worth, like the way they treat others.

Here's another question: Are you starstruck with beautiful people? Do you think people are amazing or want to be like them just because they're beautiful? It's easy to play into our culture's way of thinking. Look for the things that truly make people amazing – who they are, their character, their accomplishments, pursuing their dreams, working hard, humor, intelligence, serving others, etc. Then do two things: (1) Point those things out to the person and compliment them (*who says we only have to compliment people for looking good?*) and (2) Admire people for things that really matter.

Here are some examples of compliments that have nothing to do with beauty: "Wow, I love your ambition! You are going to do great things in life." "You are the sweetest person; I love how much you care for everyone around you." "You are really hardworking; I'm impressed with how much effort you put into your job!" "You are so creative! How do you think of these ideas?" "I love spending time with you. Your friendship means the world to me." How much more meaningful are those things than just telling someone they look good?!

things YOU can do

What are you talking about with your friends? Are the conversations all about beauty, dieting, and makeup? If so, maybe you need to slowly change your topic of conversation. A great way to start changing our culture is for each of us to start conversations with our friends or even perfect strangers. Here are some things you can do to start changing yourself and/or our culture:

1. **Find the positives in yourself and focus on those things, instead of comparing yourself to others or to magazine pictures. For example, I am a very passionate person – someone who lives fully and dreams big dreams – and I love that about myself! I can focus on that instead of comparing my body to some photoshopped super model.**

2. **Check out Dove's "Evolution" video on Youtube with your friends. Talk about the unrealistic, photoshopped images of beauty we see in the media.**

3. **Do a book study on Audrey D. Braschich's book "All Made Up." It's an interesting, easy read full of information and ideas for changing our culture.**

4. **Borrow Jean Kilbourne's half hour "Killing Us Softly" video from your local library and watch it with some of your friends. You'll be laughing the whole time *and* you'll learn a ton! Then, using what you learned in the video, when you see an advertisement, try to figure out what it's trying to sell. Look closely, because there's more than just the teeth whitening strips; there's also the idea that girls need a guy to be whole, or that if you wear the right clothes you'll be wanted, etc. (Please**

note that although I love this video, it may be inappropriate viewing for some.)

5. Join – or start – a branch of "The Body Project." Two amazing young women I met at Palm Beach Atlantic University started a branch on their campus to talk about healthy body image. By the end of the semester, all the girls participating were rating their body image more positively than in the beginning of the semester.

There are changes you can make and people you can help, right in your circle of influence. Start talking about these issues. Girls need to hear that they don't have to look like the models, because not even models are "perfect" enough. We need to live life as ourselves, comfortable in our own skin, and knowing we are fully lovable as we are.

Miss Indie, I'm out. Transforming my culture, I'm in! Together we can change the world.

what about you?

Does any of this make you mad? I hope so! What are some things you can do to change our culture?

Now don't get me wrong – I have nothing against beauty or pageants or looking cute or even using teeth whitening strips. However, we need to be careful not to buy into our culture's obsession with perfection – beauty so perfect it isn't even human! Beauty does not define our worth, even though our culture acts like it does. So here's the next foothold I found:

<u>Foothold #6: Start a conversation about beauty in the media.</u>

Our media is image-driven and all about perfection. We think we should look like the models we see in the magazines, but not even the models themselves actually look like those pictures. Start talking about this, as well as looking more critically at the advertisements and TV shows you're watching. What messages are they trying to sell you? Let's raise awareness and change our world!

Until next time,
Tiffany Dawn

Tiffany's Coffeehouse:

www.theinsatiablequestforbeauty.com

Check out the link to "8: Caramel Macchiato." Hear what my friend Sierra has to say about body image and her own journey to accepting herself, as someone who has been in the media! I also asked a graphic designer friend to Photoshop a picture of me, to show how much Photoshop can change an image. You can see that online. The song on my CD that relates with today's topic is called "This Is Beauty." It challenges our culture's perception of beauty!

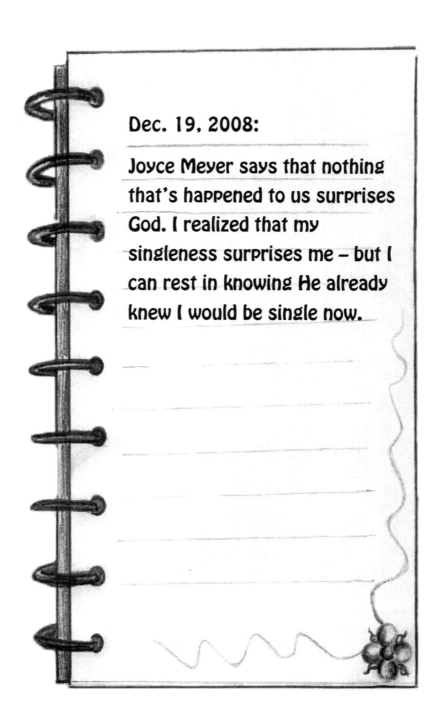

Dec. 19, 2008:

Joyce Meyer says that nothing that's happened to us surprises God. I realized that my singleness surprises me – but I can rest in knowing He already knew I would be single now.

Coffee Date #9:

This is about to get really refreshing, so I'll go with a chai latte. What are you having?

Boys, Boys, Boys

**"Staring at you taking off your makeup
Wondering why you even put it on
I know you think you do
But baby you don't need it
I wish that you could see
What I see when it's gone"**
~Rascal Flatts, "Fast Cars and Freedom"[1]

As much as it kills me to admit it, I was a girl who desperately wanted to get married. Let me be honest: I basically made wallpaper out of wedding magazines. I'd say I was a little boy crazy! It was like I thought my life would be fuller or more complete or something, like I would have more worth if I had a ring on my finger, *like it would mean someone wanted me.* So when my first boyfriend told me I wasn't pretty enough, it really messed with my head. I had always pictured being married by the time I was 20, and by 2007, I was a year overdue – probably because I wasn't pretty enough.

Overall, I was doing better with giving up my quest. For example, I read Joyce Meyer's book <u>Approval Addiction</u> and realized I was absolutely addicted to people approving of me; I couldn't be content with myself if people didn't give me that approval. My friends were encouraging me to be myself and not be afraid of what people thought. Every once in awhile I'd have moments where I found that mysterious "self" person somewhere inside me, though it was particularly difficult to "be myself" around guys.

The messed-up thoughts about my body and food lingered, though they had definitely lessened significantly. I had gained some weight due to all the amazing chocolate in Australia, and I didn't like being heavier, but I took comfort in knowing that I was loved anyway, no matter what I weighed. The problem was, just because I knew *God* loved me no matter what I looked like, didn't convince me that a *guy* would ever fall in love with me if I wasn't perfect.

As much as I pretended to be independent and not interested in a relationship, it was all a cover-up. I was afraid guys wouldn't like me back because I didn't think I was pretty enough. If people found out that I liked someone but he didn't reciprocate, then I'd feel like a failure. I was usually the one ending things by giving the cold shoulder or walking away first. No matter how serious the guy seemed, I was sure he'd lose interest sooner or later. (Probably sooner.) So if I walked away before he had a chance to end things (or start things, for that matter), no one would know I failed. My plan may have kept me safe from embarrassment, but it also isolated me behind walls so thick no guy could break through or even see who I was beneath the surface – and isn't my heart what he should fall in love with? I wrote a song about it that said:

If you saw me, would you want me?
If you knew me, would you still be here?
I guess I don't know

Have you ever felt like that? As though it's safer to not let anyone get too close, or that you're just not good enough to be loved? I figured that if I was prettier, if I could get back to my lowest weight, *then* I would be good enough. Or would I? Maybe I would never feel good enough...

Oh, one other thing. The guys I liked had to be *hot*. I didn't have the confidence to get to know a guy just because I liked who he was. He had to look good too because if he didn't, in my mind that also meant I failed. I was sure people would assume I wasn't pretty enough to get a good-looking guy, and that was *not* okay with me. That's totally shallow, but it was all part of my master plan to "protect" myself. In theory, I guess I felt badly for expecting a guy to look like Ken but still love me for my less-than-Barbie looks. Then again, what was I supposed to do – date someone who wasn't 6'3" tall, dark, and handsome? *No way!*

And then I met Karl.

karl*
*name has been changed
to protect the innocent and all that jazz

Karl wasn't anything special to look at, or at least I didn't think so. He just wasn't my type; he wasn't tall enough. I mean, come on! I'm 5'8" too when I'm wearing heels, and I am *not* giving up my heels!

I was studying abroad in Australia when I walked into his church for the first time. He was playing drums and our eyes met for an instant before I looked away. After the service, I was introduced to him and chatted for a short while, excusing myself as soon as possible so I could browse the room for a good-looking guy. You know, someone 6'3" tall, dark, and handsome – not some imposter with red hair and a whopping 68 inches of height!

Some time passed, and Karl and I became good friends. I was challenged by his walk with the Lord, his ambition, and his contagious passion. His stories of sharing Jesus' love with thousands of high school and college students convicted me.

One night we were hanging out with a few friends in the wee hours of the morning, when I walked a little distance away from the rest of the group so I could lay on the ground and look up at the stars. I was humming Misty Edward's song "Eternity" as I felt the presence of God encapsulating me and the tugging of eternity placed in my heart.

Karl walked over and sat down beside me. "What are you singing?"

"Eternity," I breathed.

After a pause he asked, "Did you write it?"

"No, but I wish I did. This one Misty Edwards wrote. It goes like this…" and I sang it for him, leaving us silent beneath its haunting refrain.

Karl finally broke the silence. "What do you want to do with your life?"

We started talking about our dreams, and I found it interesting that his dreams seemed to line up exactly with mine. I felt like I was talking to myself in male form. And the way he talked! It was gentle and unassuming, yet brimming with barely-contained passion.

"Ca-a-an you fee-ee-eel the lo-o-ove toni-i-ight?" I heard faint voices singing from a distance, and rolled my eyes. Seriously, you'd think we were in high school, not college.

As we walked back to the residence halls, he picked up his pace so we were walking out of the others' earshot. I heard his voice softly saying, "Tu eres la chica mas bonita del mundo."

I giggled, "I took Spanish, but don't remember much. What does that mean?"

A few weeks later he told me that it meant, "You are the most beautiful girl in the world." (One of his many Spanish pickup lines.) At the time, however, he was being annoying and wouldn't translate for me. He just left me with a cute little smirk playing around the corners of his mouth.

"Mom, he's really awesome," I said over the phone, "but I'm just not attracted to him. He's not tall enough."

"Tiffany," not even the phone lines could block her bluntness, "I think you need to get over your pride."

As Karl started dropping by more often, and my heart for some reason started pounding whenever I would see him, my friends teased me. "You like him, just admit it!"

"No, I don't!" I'd pound my words into the air. "Once and for all, I'm not interested!"

"Then why are you worrying so much about what you're going to wear when you hang out with him tonight?" (He had called me to go to the mall – just me, not the other girls.)

"Because you never know who you're going to see at the mall."

But I knew I was in denial, and after a few months I stopped trying to fake it. Truthfully, I was falling for Karl. I found myself drawn to *who he was*, rather than just the surface appearances. We had so much fun together, some of the memories I cherish most. Sure there were things that annoyed me about him, but overall, it slowly dawned on me that I wanted to spend my life with someone like Karl. When I left him behind in Australia, I would be leaving a piece of my heart as well.

One night he was preaching at our young adults group. I had heard him speak before and had always been amazed, but for some reason this time it struck a chord in my heart. As he was speaking with an intoxicating mixture of zeal and wisdom, I found myself appreciating him for who he was. That night was like a window into his soul, and everything I saw within him was exactly what I wanted.

That was the night I fell in love with him.

the scrapbook you

When I fell head-over-knees for Karl, I couldn't tell whether or not he was attractive to anyone else. I was so drawn to him – all of him – that I could no longer figure out whether or not he was handsome or would be considered "arm candy." I remember staring at pictures of him trying to figure out if he was cute or if it was just me, but all I knew was that I found him extremely attractive – as a whole person. That's what it's like to truly love someone. You love everything about them. You are so drawn to them that you can't separate who they are inside from who they are outside; it's all one big, wonderful, and whole package.

Some guys separate girls into pieces. They see your chest or your butt or your great personality or your passion for good causes, but they're not seeing *you*. Those are the kinds of guys I don't want to be with. I want someone who sees all of me and doesn't run away. I want someone who sees me and is drawn to the scrapbook me, from every angle, not the snapshot me. After all, if I, the queen of shallowness, could fall in love with the less-than-perfect Karl, then maybe – *just maybe* – someone could fall in love with the less-than-perfect me.

On the other hand, how many great guys had I walked right past as though they were invisible just because they didn't measure up to my 6'3" height requirement? Meeting Karl made me realize that I want to be someone who sees a guy for everything he is and falls in love with the scrapbook him. Who am I to expect a guy to see me just as I am, with my imperfections, and love me, yet simultaneously I will only date a guy who is perfect? Something needed to change.

Leaving Australia was horrible. It was as if I had reached the end of something beautiful with Karl before I ever found the beginning of it. What do you do when all that's left are *ifs* and *could have beens*? There was so much unrealized potential; it felt like I was just up and walking away from my destiny.

I came back to the U.S. and Karl moved to Japan to plant a church. My goal? Of course, to move to Japan and help him out! (My sister Liyah thought I was just chasing another boy, but I was convinced it was different this time.) I went to an interview for a job that would send me to Japan. I'd been hanging all my hopes on this interview, and I totally rocked it! All I had to do was wait for the call.

But the call never came. Only a letter saying they had chosen another candidate.

I couldn't believe it!! That was *not* meant to happen! I was sure it was God's will for me to go over there, work, help with the church, and marry Karl. What happened?? After my interview Karl wrote me to see if I'd gotten the job. I had to admit I hadn't, and so I didn't know when or *if* I'd move to Japan. A couple months later, Karl was dating his future wife.

I'm sure you've had those moments when you really liked someone only to find out he decided to go for someone else. (And then you pull up her picture on Facebook and you and all your friends sit around critiquing her until you feel better about yourself and reaffirmed that he was an idiot not to choose you, right? I used to do that.) I felt like I was going to throw up! *If only I'd been prettier he wouldn't have forgotten about me!* (Not that living on opposite sides of the world had anything to do with it. I'm not very logical about boys.) And once again, I felt like a failure. That horrible feeling, my self-fulfilled prophecy: I couldn't keep anyone's attention.

so what do the guys have to say?

I could only hope that someday someone would love the scrapbook me, but it was easy to lose hope. It was easy to focus on the negatives in myself, feel unlovable, and be afraid that I would never get or keep a guy's attention. So I asked a few quality men what they were looking for in a relationship, and how someone like me (a.k.a., not the prettiest woman in the world) could get and keep a guy's attention. Here's what they said:

> **Isaac (my brother): Even if a woman isn't the prettiest person, she can still be the most beautiful woman you know if she has the right characteristics. To Isaac, those characteristics are when a woman truly cares about God and others. He says, "If a guy only has one reason to talk to you and care about you, it better not be your makeup."**

113

Andrew (my brother): Confidence is extremely attractive to guys, so don't assume you're ugly and act like it. To Andrew the most attractive features of a woman are her ability to make you laugh and if her eyes show her passions. He says, "If a guy only likes you for your looks, he will only like you till he finds someone who looks better. Skip your makeup one day or don't do your hair and see if he is still in love with you."

Jonny: When you are beautiful inside, through your character, personality, etc., you become attractive. If you lack that inward beauty, even if you are outwardly beautiful, you become less attractive. He said, "Guys that are worthwhile will go beyond that [skin-deep beauty] and will see you for who you are inside. In his eyes, you will be the most beautiful girl in the world because of what he sees in you. Don't strive for physical beauty. If you love Jesus with abandon and are content in who you are, perfect beauty will be yours."

Eric: "Present yourself with confidence. In my opinion the most important thing to a lot of guys is for a woman to have confidence in herself."

Jonathan: He's looking for honesty, a real relationship with a genuine person. He concluded, "If the guy runs, it's obvious right off the bat that it isn't going to be a meaningful relationship. Not worth spending time with someone if it isn't honest."

Nate: Physical attraction is important – you can't get around that. But that doesn't mean someone should expect the other person to look a certain way or be the person of their dreams. He said, "It's the job of any guy...to affirm the women that they have in their lives. Don't waste your time with guys who you always have to try to impress and who never love you for who you are." He said it's also very attractive if a girl is confident and comfortable in her own skin.

Kyle: The first thing people notice off the bat is physical appearance, but then beauty becomes many different things – coming in the form of personalities, humor, caring interactions, etc. Confidence is important in all of life and comes from within you. Find confidence in areas of life where you succeed and "then that just builds you up as a person and bleeds into the other aspects of your life, which you're more sensitive about or more self-conscious about."

Justin: "It's not a girl's job to keep a guy's attention. If you don't keep a person's attention, you probably shouldn't be with them. You don't want that guy. Trying to keep his attention isn't love; it's tricks and manipulation. When you're dating, you're not putting on a play; you're relating to a human being. You should be with someone whose character is similar to your own. Looks aren't going to do it; it's gotta be character. I like it when a girl takes care of herself, don't get me wrong. But I don't care if my girlfriend has makeup on or not when I go over there."

Joel: "It's not so much that guys are attracted to girls who are attractive; it's that guys are attracted to people who take care of themselves. It's not so much about having the right look; it's about taking care of yourself." He explained that what "taking care of yourself" meant was having hobbies, friends, being healthy (NOT obsessed with beauty).

I was encouraged to hear that quality men weren't obsessed with a woman looking like some fantasy; they just wanted someone who was real, honest, confident, and who took care of herself so she could look *her* best for him (not "the best" of some fake ideal). They also wanted to fall in love with who she was inside – the scrapbook her – rather than with a perfect body. That seemed doable to me…

when he goes for someone else

Time went on, and they say it heals all things.

The next summer I was seeing this guy whom I'll call Jake. He was nothing like Karl. I mean, he was nice and cute and all, but I wasn't in love with him. I was trying to force myself to go out with someone, because I thought that would help me get over my fears (kind of selfish, I know). When Jake asked me to be his girlfriend, I told him I wanted to keep the relationship at a casual dating level. That casual level was hard enough for me because I felt like I was going to puke every time I saw him. It wasn't a nervous "butterflies in your stomach" feeling; it was an *"I'm scared to death of letting someone get close to me"* nausea. When he moved 20 hours away for college, we tried to keep it going, only to have him call me one night saying, "This isn't really working. I'm just not feeling a spark here."

There it was happening to me all over again! Why did I *never* give anyone a reason to stay? Why couldn't I be prettier? If I was prettier, surely I'd be married by now! I called my best guy friend, totally freaking out.

"Justin, I can't give anyone a reason to stay! Jake doesn't like me either. I'm not pretty enough. Jeez, if I had known he was going to break up with me, I would have broken up with him first! Not that it was even breaking up, 'cause I told him I wouldn't be his girlfriend. So there!"

Justin started laughing. *(The nerve!)* "Tiffany, you didn't even like him! This is God's blessing. If I had to choose – out of every girl in the world – who I was going to marry, I'd never be able to make the choice. Just look at it as God narrowing down your options. It's a good thing it didn't work out, cause it means you're one person closer to figuring out who you're going to be with."

He continued, "Every girl I've gotten to know, either I've known or she's known that we weren't supposed to be together. When she's the one who knows, I don't take that as rejection; I just take that as God guiding me."

I was still seething, but eventually the truth of his words made sense. Why was I freaking out? Not every guy would like me. Everyone likes different things; I like dark-haired guys and my friend Ashley likes blond boys. That doesn't mean one of them is cuter than the other, it just means we're attracted to different things. Some guys would like me, and some wouldn't. That didn't mean there was something wrong with me or that I would never find a boyfriend. In fact, it was probably a good thing that not every guy liked me, because I'm extremely indecisive and would never be able to make up my mind! I would just have to let go of the guys who were not interested, instead of trying to hold onto something that would never happen. As Anne of Green Gables said, I only need one boy in his right mind, not a string of them going crazy for me.[2]

After that conversation with Justin, one of my friends said, "Wow, Jake was an idiot! One day he'll find out what he was missing." I chuckled, and then unrecognizable words came out of my mouth: "Actually, I don't think he will. We weren't right for each other, so why would he be missing out? We're both great people, but if we're not right for each other then no one's missing anything." (And then I thought, *Who the heck is speaking through my mouth right now??*)

you are valuable

For some strange reason I thought that if I got enough guys to like me and date me, I would prove my beauty to the world. It seemed like the women who had the coolness factor of five thousand always had a boyfriend, so of course I should too. But when I stopped to think about it, why would I give my heart away to guy after guy just to make me feel better about myself? Why would I throw myself after hot guys just for the pick-me-up of feeling beautiful until one of us threw the other away? I am worth so much more than that! (And so are they!)

In March 2007 I wrote this in my journal:

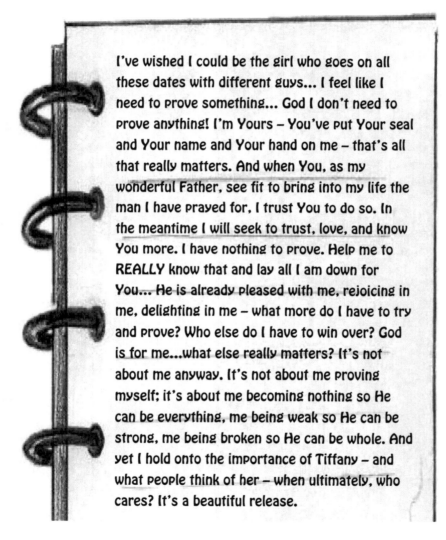

I've wished I could be the girl who goes on all these dates with different guys... I feel like I need to prove something... God I don't need to prove anything! I'm Yours – You've put Your seal and Your name and Your hand on me – that's all that really matters. And when You, as my wonderful Father, see fit to bring into my life the man I have prayed for, I trust You to do so. In the meantime I will seek to trust, love, and know You more. I have nothing to prove. Help me to REALLY know that and lay all I am down for You... He is already pleased with me, rejoicing in me, delighting in me – what more do I have to try and prove? Who else do I have to win over? God is for me...what else really matters? It's not about me anyway. It's not about me proving myself; it's about me becoming nothing so He can be everything, me being weak so He can be strong, me being broken so He can be whole. And yet I hold onto the importance of Tiffany – and what people think of her – when ultimately, who cares? It's a beautiful release.

Once again the healing current of time rolled on. Each year was another step in my awakening to the fact that having a boyfriend would not increase or prove my worth. Instead of going after guys because they were hot, I started keeping my eye out for a guy that I really liked because of who he was. I was single for two years because the only guys I liked didn't like me back, and I wasn't going to date someone I didn't like just for the added security of having a boyfriend. I started to see that my heart was a treasure that should be won. So if I didn't know any guys who would be worth my time, I didn't give them my time.

When I was seventeen, I wasn't willing to wait for someone better, and so I dated a guy I never should have dated. If I were to relive that, I would have sent him packing before we ever went out. It kills me to see young women, some of whom are my dear friends, selling themselves short. They give their hearts and bodies away to men who don't deserve them, putting up with guys treating them poorly, because these women don't realize how valuable they are. They don't realize they are worth more than that!

If I could share anything with you, it would be this: You are a treasure. Your heart is priceless. If a guy doesn't realize that, and if he treats you like crap, don't give him the time of day. You don't need some old boyfriend to give you confidence; you can be confident right now even if you're single. And ironically that kind of life and confidence will draw the heart of a good man. My worth is not measured by the hotness factor of the guys I date. My value does not come from having a string of boyfriends. My confidence does not rest on how many guys check me out. I am a beloved daughter of the King. That is the only solid foundation on which I can base my confidence. What the Creator of the universe thinks of me is more important than what anyone in this world thinks, and having a long string of boyfriends won't impress Him.

Don't date to find your worth, because you already have your worth. You are already valuable, and you are too precious to throw your heart at guys who don't treat you like a daughter of the King. Your worth is wrapped up in the love of Jesus Christ, not in boys.

oh yeah...they're valuable too!

On the other hand, guys are valuable too! Over the years, my mom has repeatedly told me, "Tiffany, you're not being fair to him; you're leading him on." I seriously had a hard time believing her. I pretty much thought all guys were just like my ex-boyfriend and deserved a little ego-busting. Now I'm starting to see how wrong I was.

Sometimes in my attempt to feel better about myself, I flirted with guys I had no intention of ever going out with. I enjoyed the way I felt when they paid attention to me, but gave no thought as to how my actions could affect their emotions, or how much I would have hated if a guy treated me that way. My mom was right; I *was* being unfair to them. (Apparently guys *do* have blood running through their veins, and hearts that can be broken – who would have thought?) Theoretically, I now realize that a relationship isn't about what you can *get*, but about what you can *give*. I'm still working on taking that realization from my head to my actions.

Hopefully you know this already and are horrified at the way I used to act. But just in case you're like me and unwittingly have been a "man-eater," remember that the guys have value too. Let's be careful in the way we treat guys. Just as much as they shouldn't treat us like crap, we also shouldn't treat them like crap. They are our "brothers" in the family of God, and I know I wouldn't want girls messing with *my* brothers!

satisfied

So you're valuable (and so are guys). Your worth is found in Jesus, not in boys. At this point it can be easy to think that even if we're confident, single women, we are still missing out on being fully satisfied. I thought that once I got married, I'd be even more confident and never feel lonely again!

One day I was having coffee with one of my married friends when she told me, "My husband can't satisfy all my needs. When I look to him to satisfy me, I get frustrated and lonely, because only Jesus can fully satisfy my heart."

That stopped me cold! All this time, even though I was mostly satisfied in Jesus, I still thought that the companionship of marriage would prevent me from ever getting lonely again. Yet here was a friend with a beautiful marriage and wonderful husband – and she still felt lonely if she wasn't being filled up with Jesus! So if I couldn't be happy now, after marriage that same dissatisfaction I had before would return.

Love often becomes another insatiable quest, another place girls look for satisfaction. But according to my married friends, no guy can satisfy our hearts for the long run. So instead of waiting for our lives to start when we meet Mr. Right, we need to stop waiting! The best thing we can do right now is become whole people, satisfied in the only One who can ever fully satisfy our hearts.

I'm not saying it's always easy to do this, but it won't get any easier once we're married, so we may as well start practicing now! When you feel lonely, that's okay. It's a normal part of life. But remember it won't disappear forever just because you're in a relationship. At some point it will resurface and you'll need to know what to do with it. So begin taking that loneliness to God and finding yourself in Him.

December 21, 2008: This loneliness is suffocating and makes me want to scream or explode. Sometimes I feel so alone it's like I'm holding my breath. Jesus help me to find myself in You.

hope

Fast forward to 2010 – the year I started dating my second boyfriend. It was different than anything I'd ever experienced. Once again I was scared to death and for awhile held him at arm's length, but when I let him come a little closer, it was healing.

He loved me for who I was. He loved when I'd be so crazy I thought he'd never want to see me again. He loved the dreams in my heart that seemed to intimidate other guys. And he had emotions; he wanted a deep connection in the relationship; he didn't deserve to have his ego busted. It was weird!

One day especially stands out to me. I was feeling gross and hadn't done my makeup that day, so when we planned to get together at the last minute, I texted him, "Just to warn you, I didn't do my makeup, didn't shower, and am wearing a sweatshirt." He wrote back, "I'm sure you look great, but you don't have to try to impress me. I don't care what you're wearing; I just can't wait to see you!" (*That's nice, but he hasn't seen me yet.*) When I walked in the door he greeted me with a huge hug and asked incredulously, "What were you talking about? You look great!"

I started to believe him. I never felt like I wasn't good enough for him. Instead, I felt like I was more than enough. During that year, I learned how to be myself, let out the craziness, and embrace life. I loved dressing up for our dates, but I also loved the way I could show up in sweatpants and a ponytail and he would love me just as much. It contradicted my old mindset.

As is the story of my life thus far, that relationship didn't last either. We spent the last month praying and talking with our pastor and his wife. We just didn't feel like we were quite right for each other. Some important things didn't match up, so we decided to end our relationship. But instead of leaving with a broken, rejected heart, I left more whole than before, and he said he did too.

I left realizing that I could be loved for me, including (*not despite*) all my messy imperfections. I left with a newfound confidence. I left with a taste of what a good relationship is like, and with excitement for how awesome my marriage would be someday! I left with *hope*.

I wrote a song when we broke up, which says:

When have I been one to go with whatever's comfortable?
When have I been one to fear the unknown?
My God has a plan for me, a future and a hope
This I know, this I know

what about you?

My God has a plan for me – and it's a good plan.

I'm twenty-five, single, and confident. Even though I haven't yet found a guy to share my life with, that doesn't mean I won't. It might take awhile, *but my heart is worth the wait*. Although I am looking forward to the day my beautiful desire for a husband comes true, I am living life fully, satisfied in my relationship with Jesus and enjoying the friends around me. Each year that goes by, more of my friends meet Mr. Right and get married. I am so excited for them! But I wouldn't trade my singleness for the world. Right now, this is where I'm supposed to be. I couldn't see that before; I thought being single meant I wasn't good enough. Really it's all a part of God's plan for my life, and I am so excited for the adventure He has in store!

Where are you right now? Single, dating, married, divorced? Wherever you are, I am so excited for the plans God has for you! Sometimes we can't see it, but when we give our love lives over to Him, He has good plans in store for us!

There is so much more I wish I had time to share with you. I would talk until our drinks grew cold and we were literally thrown out of the coffee shop. In fact, I've started writing another book all about relationships and finding confidence when we're single, because you just can't talk about everything in one measly coffee date. But for now, remember that you are valuable. Your worth comes because Jesus Christ died for you – that's how far He went to pursue your heart. Being with Mr. Perfect will not fulfill you, so learn to live a full and confident life right now, whether or not you're in a relationship. There may be plenty more times when the both of us will like guys only to have them go off with someone else, but that's okay. As we come to terms with that and realize it is no reflection on whether or not we will one day find someone who loves us, we can be at peace with it. And lastly, have hope. As you love the Lord with all your heart and find wholeness in Him, you will find there is no greater joy than to be in the center of His will, and He will complete that perfect will in your life. So here's the next foothold:

Foothold #7: Live with confidence in and out of relationships; your worth does not depend on dating cute guys.

My quest for beauty began as a reason to capture a guy's heart. The next step of my climb was realizing that beauty would not grant me the love story I dreamed of, nor would that love story satisfy completely – as I had hoped. Instead of waiting for a guy to begin my life with, I began to live fully and confidently right now, knowing my worth was unchangeable, coming from the love Jesus Christ showed me. As I have come to know His love more and more, I have come to fully believe that one day He will fulfill this desire of my heart for a man to share my life with, and when that day comes I will be a whole person, already complete and satisfied.

Until next time,
Tiffany Dawn

Tiffany's Coffeehouse:

www.theinsatiablequestforbeauty.com

Check out the link to "9: Chai Latte." I interviewed some more guys, asking them what they were looking for in a girl, and then compiled it into a video. Then there is a deleted scene called "Why I Threw Out My List," about what I'm looking for in a guy, and a recording of the song I wrote for Karl, called "Other Side of the World." Lastly, the song on my CD that goes along with today's chapter is titled "Someday." (It's my princess song. And it sparkles.)

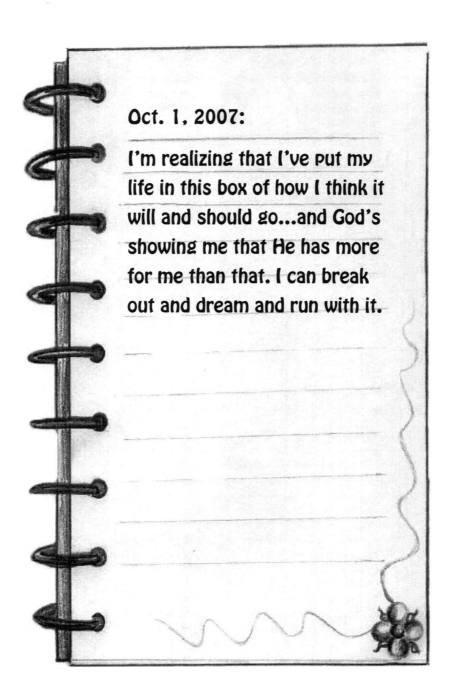

Oct. 1, 2007:

I'm realizing that I've put my life in this box of how I think it will and should go...and God's showing me that He has more for me than that. I can break out and dream and run with it.

Coffee Date #10:

**I'll have a pumpkin flavored latte today.
Doesn't it remind you of Thanksgiving?
What are you having?**

Getting Over the Quest

**"I have found that among its other benefits,
giving liberates the soul of the giver."**
~Maya Angelou₁

Have you ever tried to get over a guy by focusing on how much you are over him? You and your girlfriends sit around giving yourself pep talks. "He's not worth it." "A total jerk." "You could do so much better." "He wasn't even all that cute!" It's a great trick…until your friends leave and you're sitting all alone. If you're anything like me, that's when you break down over a box of chocolates and a chick flick, and realize you're nowhere near over him.

For a long time I tried this technique. I'd critique the guy's every flaw, not realizing that while I was trying to talk myself out of liking him, I was continuing to think about him. The trick was backfiring. I was so focused on not wanting him, that I was still focused on him.

When we focus too intently on ourselves, we become more easily caught up in our quests. The secret to getting over a guy is the same secret to taking another step up the mountainside of freedom from our quests: Stop constantly thinking about getting over it, and instead start thinking about something else. Instead of thinking about not wanting it, look for ways to give back to the world around you, things to "distract" you in a sense, until you stop craving beauty. You can't just get rid of one quest; you have to replace it with something else – something healthy – a quest that truly satisfies. Here are a few ways to do this…

your place in the great adventure

I love meeting women and hearing what they want to do with their lives. From my friend Kellie who wants to write children's books, to my friend Hannah who wants to create a documentary, to my sister Liyah who is in med school, to my sister Amy who writes incredible, classical-sounding piano pieces, to my Mom who loves teaching science classes, it amazes me how unique each person's desires are as they fill a need in the world.

As much as our passions can fill a need in the world, they can also save us from drowning in our quests. I can't tell you how many times the fact that I am writing this book and speaking with young women has been the encouragement I needed to keep going. There are still occasions when I am tempted to run back to my obsession with beauty, but I have something else I want more. I have realized that the quest only leaves me empty and broken; but I know where to find fullness of life, and I want to share that truth with other women.

We each need a purpose in life. Finding my purpose gave me another outlet for my emotions and energy; it gave me something else to focus on and work toward. Having a goal I am working toward has helped me overcome my feelings of inadequacy and insecurity. It has given me a higher reason to live.

Today God is bringing into my life opportunities to do the very things I have longed to do my whole life. I have a passion burning in my heart to reach young women with this message of freedom in the Lord, and here I am, writing this book and speaking to young people...who would have thought?

One day I walked out onto a stage to lead 1,500 teens and adults in worship, and the short walk to the piano felt like hours. I was overcome with the thought that if I had gone my own way, followed my own quest, I would not be there. I would still be exhausted from climbing my crooked staircase. My quest would have led to destruction, not to fullness of life.

I had to close my eyes while playing that day because I was so close to tears. Every time I opened my eyes, I choked up, because when I saw those teens pressed up to the front of the stage, my heart ached to pour my life out for them. "God, this is where I want to be," I prayed. "If I could just be right here, pouring my life out for them, then I would be doing what I was made to do." There is nothing like doing what you were made to do. There is nothing like sharing the adventure of life with the Lord.

Use this time to find your place in that great adventure. Pursue something you are interested in. It could be anything from tutoring at a homework help program to playing in a band, reading every classic out there to traveling abroad, joining a sports team to running for class president, interior decorating to interning in politics. But whatever you choose to do, do it with excellence. Practice, work at it, and enjoy it. Now is the time in life to pursue the things you are interested in. Let that pursuit be a healthy outlet to take your eyes off yourself as you pour yourself into something bigger than your life.

serve others

Mrs. DuPré, my mentor and pastor's wife, once told me that if I want to be comfortable in social situations, I should focus on making other people feel comfortable instead of focusing on how I feel. It works! Being absorbed in the other person and learning about him/her causes me to forget my insecurities, while gaining friends. Look around you and find the good, beautiful, and interesting things in each person you meet. Make it a goal to sincerely compliment three people a day. Pretty soon you'll find it becoming second nature to compliment everyone you meet! From there, start to make time for service.

Maya Angelou once said, "I've learned that people will forget what you said, people will forget what you did, but people will never forget how you made them feel."[2] If I could revise that beautiful quote for this book, it would read:

People will forget what you looked like
People will forget what you wore
But people will never forget how you made them feel.
So if you want to be unforgettable
Love passionately,
Care unconditionally,
And serve selflessly.

Go out of your way to serve others. You could visit a soup kitchen, write holiday cards to children with terminal illnesses, find a place to volunteer at your church, visit elderly people living in assisted living homes, participate in breast cancer walks, or rake your neighbor's lawn. There are many ways to serve, and many needs all around us. Serving not only helps others, but it also takes our eyes off of our quests.

Another kind of service is to share your story with others. God loves to take what we've been through, and use it to help others through similar struggles. Since coming out of my quest, all I want to do is talk about it. I get so stinking mad at the way the media portrays women and the pressure to look perfect, and I want to tell people they don't have to look a certain way! So every chance I get, I'm talking with people about these issues, trying to raise awareness, and to do something so other girls don't go down the same path I did. If this overemphasis on beauty makes you mad – *good!* Let's do something about it.

what about you?

What are your interests and passions? Is there something you've done to take your eyes off of yourself? What are some practical things you can do to "distract" yourself from this beauty focus?

Mother Teresa said that until we're living for others, our life "is not worth living."[3] As long as I was focused on myself, my life revolved around my insecurities. When I started paying attention to others, I found passion, purpose, and a real reason for living! Here's the next foothold:

Foothold #8: Take your eyes off of yourself and focus on others, giving back to the world around you.

It's easy to get so caught up in finding freedom that we are still focused on our quest. Being others-focused can help shift our eyes so we don't drown in our quest while trying to find freedom. Here's your challenge: Compliment three people today, make plans to serve in some way, and find a hobby – something you enjoy doing – to pour your energy into. Start to find your place in the great adventure!

Until next time,
Tiffany Dawn

Tiffany's Coffeehouse:

www.theinsatiablequestforbeauty.com

Check out the link to "10: Pumpkin Flavored Latte."
I'm going to introduce you to my friend Alyson today – a
young woman who is making a difference in the world and
burning with a passion that gives her confidence. I included
a list of some service ideas, and the song on my CD for
today is called "Who Will Go."

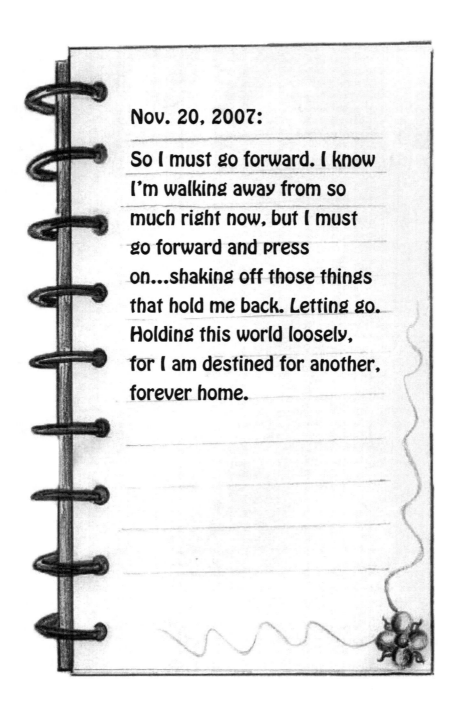

Nov. 20, 2007:

So I must go forward. I know I'm walking away from so much right now, but I must go forward and press on...shaking off those things that hold me back. Letting go. Holding this world loosely, for I am destined for another, forever home.

Coffee Date #11:

My favorite obsession for my favorite chapter: Raspberry chai! What are you having?

Unlocking Confidence

"If I find in myself
Desires nothing in this world can satisfy
Then of course I'll conclude
That I - I was not made for here"
~Brooke Fraser, "C.S. Lewis Song"[1]

I'm about to let you in on a little secret: I am *obsessed* with spies. I used to think I wanted to be one, only to realize that I wouldn't be able to tell anyone about my "glorious" missions. What's the fun in that? Oh, and I hate danger in real life. So I decided I should play a spy in a movie.

Next to daydreaming about becoming a spy-actress, one of my favorite things to do is meet incredible women and ask them to get coffee with me so I can interrogate them. I feel like a secret agent – like Sarah Walker in the TV series *Chuck* – going undercover and asking pointed questions to figure out what these ladies' secrets are to living as women of God. I then take confidential, coded notes by journaling anything they said that stood out in my mind.

While in Australia, I met one of the sweetest ladies ever. Her walk with God and love for everyone around her intrigued me, so one day I invited myself over for dinner. I came with my usual list of questions and journal to take notes.

We talked about God, boys, dreams, boys, church, and more about boys. Somewhere toward the end of our chat, we were talking about feeling beautiful, and I asked her, "So does it work?"

"Does what work?"

"Do you really feel confident and beautiful most of the time now, by believing God says you're beautiful?"

She paused, looking off thoughtfully as I tried to read her expression like a true spy.

"No," she finally looked back at me, "I don't. I'm always trying to convince myself and remember that I'm beautiful. I think it's a battle that we as women will have to fight for the rest of our lives."

I couldn't breathe for a second and completely forgot my Secret Agent persona. *The rest of my life??? I may as well give up now!* I sat there, my pen suspended in midair, which Sarah on *Chuck* would *never* do.

And that's when it came to me: *Maybe we're fighting the wrong battle.*

Maybe it doesn't matter whether or not we feel beautiful, maybe we don't have to fight to feel that way all the time. Maybe beauty isn't a good place for our confidence to be. Maybe there's something greater that can give us confidence, whether or not we feel beautiful. Maybe we really would be fighting that battle the rest of our lives, simply because it's the wrong battle.

I grew up with a misconstrued understanding of beauty. The beauty I saw in society had to do with perfect appearances. The beauty I saw in the Christian church had to do with perfect character – or at least that's how I perceived it. And in both society and the church, I thought the key to being confident was to have beauty. If I could just feel pretty outside or inside, I would be confident. Even those who told me God said I was beautiful made me think, "If that's true, then does He love me just because He thinks I'm beautiful? Is the secret to confidence thinking God says I'm beautiful? The key is still beauty in that equation! We're still focusing on beauty, as though it is the most important thing, *as though we have to feel beautiful to be confident!*"

But that day in Australia I came to the best conclusion I ever have on my secret spy missions: "I'm fighting a losing battle. Why? Because I'm fighting the *wrong* battle."

The confidence I have found and the premise on which this book and my seminar are based *have nothing to do with beauty*. My confidence does not depend on the way I look or how good of a person I am, and I'm not going to tell you the key is believing God thinks you're beautiful. Why? Because I believe our confidence should leave beauty entirely out of the equation. Oddly enough, I also believe our confidence should leave *ourselves* entirely out of the equation.

I can find confidence in being a beloved daughter of the King. That's who I am on my good days and on my bad days, whether or not I feel beautiful. It never changes. I know who I am, and I know that I am loved no matter what. That's where I have found my confidence over the past few years, and I have grown into a freedom I never knew before.

But recently I felt like there was something missing, a key that would unlock a deeper confidence. I hadn't been able to put a finger on why that was until I read Leslie Ludy's book Set-Apart Femininity. Suddenly the problem became crystal clear: I was focusing on myself, as if I was the most important thing in the world!

Focusing on ourselves almost seems like the right thing to do. In fact, it's *the* thing to do in our culture. Everything is about us, whether it's finding the right fit jeans or the right fit church. When does our self-worship end and true worship begin?

The missing *something* I sensed was that my life was still all about me.

two seconds of fame

My friend Krysta had been raving about some book called Crazy Love by Francis Chan. Even the title sounded a little too crazy, so I was slightly hesitant to check it out when she let me borrow it. But from the first page, I was hooked.

Francis Chan wrote that our life on this earth is like being in a movie.[2] Imagine you were recruited as an "extra" character – one of many faces on the screen during a two-second scene in a feature-length movie. The movie was all about God – in the beginning God created the earth, then a whole series of events occurred (all of which were about God), then Jesus came, then a whole series of events occurred again (all of which were about God), and in the end Jesus returned. Somewhere during the second half of the movie you got to be on screen for a total of two seconds, along with several thousand other characters. You were so excited that you went and invited all your friends and family to come see this movie – which you claimed was all about you.

Francis Chan said that is how we act in our lives. Our 70ish years on earth are as short as a breath when compared with eternity. They're here, and then they're gone. And while we have those years to live, they are supposed to be all about God. *Yet we act like they are all about us.*

Let me add in a quick clarifier. As my friend Deb was reading through this chapter, she pointed out that some of us might read that last paragraph and think our life has no value. We might not "see the freedom in that statement," as Deb put it. So I want to pause a minute and make sure you remember everything we've talked about up to this point.

You are beloved! You have value! You are one of a kind and precious! The part you play in the kingdom of God is important, but it isn't for *your* glory; it's all for *Him*. There is indescribable freedom that comes when we realize that our life is not for us; it's for God. There's a bigger picture and a higher purpose. Once I learned that I was precious and loved by God, I had to learn that this life was all about Him – not about me. That understanding brought freedom that I had never known before. So bear with me, remembering that your life has an important mission: To point to Him.

beauty for a cross

As long as we are living for ourselves, beauty will continue to be critical. We will continue to feel insecure and to fight a losing battle toward joy. It's when we give up our life that we gain it, when we lose our life that we find it.

Let's go back to the second verse I shared with you on our third coffee date – the verse that was read in the church service when I quietly surrendered my quest for beauty:

"Whoever desires to come after Me, let him deny himself, and take up his cross, and follow Me. For whoever desires to save his life will lose it, but whoever loses his life for My sake and the gospel's will save it. For what will it profit a man if he gains the whole world, and loses his own soul? Or what will a man give in exchange for his soul?" (Mark 8:34-37)

I didn't fully understand why God showed me Mark 8:34 that day, but now I know. It was quite simply because He was asking me to exchange my beauty for a cross. He was not offering to give me a life of ease, fame, effortless beauty, and meanwhile allow me to feel confident in who *I* was. No, He was asking me to let go of my own life so I could find His life. He wanted me to disappear so He could appear. He wanted me to find my confidence in who *He* is, rather than in anything having to do with me.

The secret to a life of purpose, fulfillment, and confidence, is to take up your cross. It's to serve the people around you, to go out of your way to consider others to be better than yourself. Living with purpose means living every moment to glorify the Lord, and giving no thought to your own pleasure. Living with joy means giving everything you have for those who have nothing. Living with confidence means delighting yourself completely in the Lord. There is no other way to find the abundant life He came to give us than to lose ourselves in Him.

As long as beauty or you yourself are in the equation, the sum total will not be a strong, unshakeable confidence. But once you've discovered this higher purpose, once you've thrown your life over Jesus in wasteful abandon, *then* purpose, confidence, and joy will be yours – pressed down, shaken together, and spilling over.

If you want to be free from your quest for beauty, stop worrying about what other people think of you and start living a courageous life that matters in eternity. If you want to be free from your quest for beauty, stop living for yourself and start living to pour out your life for God and others. If you want to be free from your quest for beauty, then take up your cross and follow Him.

Lord, I know that You are God. I will follow You.

March 21, 2010: There's a kind of courage that comes only when we're looking to His face and allowing everything else to fade into the background.

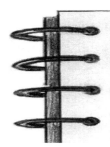

know what you're living for

I love ZOEGirl. They're these three ladies who I suspect are undercover for the CIA, because I swear they must read my journals before writing their songs. In one of my favorite songs of theirs, called "Good Girl," they wrote:

What sets you apart from everyone else
Is that you know your Savior and you know Him well [3]

This is what sets us apart: We know Who we're living for. We know our Savior, and all we can say when we see His love is, "Here I am, I will follow You." As André French sang: "What can I say, what can I do, but to offer up my life in light of you."[4]

What else can we say? When we have discovered a love as passionate as Jesus' love for us, there is nothing else we desire but to give Him everything we are.

Know what you are living for. Yes, it's a narrow road, but you should not be living for yourself or for this world's opinion of you; you should be living to know God and make Him known. There will be times when you look like a fool, when what you stand for is unpopular, and when you don't "feel" happy and motivated. But through it all, remember that this life is not for you; it is for God, the Creator and Ruler of the universe. He is the King, but He is also your Father. Live out of love for Him. I truly believe that having that higher purpose, that greater quest, is the *only way* you can walk in complete freedom from your insatiable quest. As Mrs. Parker, a family friend, once said, "It takes having your confidence in God's love for you and desiring His heart above all other allurements" to really, truly be free from society's pressure to be perfect.

Let me clarify. I am *not* talking about the "I-go-to-church" Christianity that we so often see in America. If that is the way we try to find freedom from the quest for beauty, we won't find freedom. It will not replace the quest. Freedom does not come from living a half-hearted Christian life or taking a lukewarm approach to Jesus.

Freedom comes when we count every single thing as loss for the sake of knowing Him more; when we pursue Him with all our time, heart, mind, soul, effort, motivation, and strength – with every part of who we are; when others sometimes call us crazy or over the top. *Freedom will not come if Jesus is only a part of your life; it will come when He is your life.* When you take up your cross and follow Him, making Him the center of every day you live, every breath you breathe. That, and that alone, is when freedom will come, because truly nothing else will matter to you; only having more of Jesus in your life.

141

As Paul Oakley wrote in "It's All About You" (one of my top ten favorite songs of all time):

It's all about you, Jesus
And all this is for you, for your glory and your praise
It's not about me, as if you should do things my way
You alone are God and I surrender to your way[5]

I love that song because it is a beautiful reminder of the truth: This life is not for me and it's not about me. When I take my eyes off of myself, I can see that there is a bigger picture. Whether or not I have it all together or am beautiful doesn't matter. I am not entitled to my own way in life, or to my own personal success. I don't deserve to be beautiful or to have the right clothes. My life is a gift for a purpose – that purpose being to bring God glory. I need to stop living for myself and start living for God's glory. Am I glorifying God? Am I in a growing relationship with God? Am I loving the people around me? That's what matters.

falling into place

When I started living out of this perspective, *everything* fell into place. My eating, my thoughts, my perspective on beauty, the way I saw myself, my confidence. Whatever had been missing fell into place because my life was no longer my own; it was His.

Let me share a story with you about a woman who lived this kind of life, and the confidence she gained from a life focused only on Jesus.

She didn't have a date that night. No, she was here in search of Jesus. She didn't receive honor and recognition. No, she received indignant reproaches from Jesus' closest friends, His disciples. But from Jesus she received praise. And apparently His praise was all that mattered to her.

It must have been a curious sight, this young woman walking to the door of the house where only the men were gathered, her hair softly blowing back in the evening breeze. Slightly disheveled, she clutched a breathtakingly gorgeous alabaster flask against her chest. It sparkled as she moved through the doorway and into the candlelight of the house.

She hesitated, almost holding her breath, blending in with the shadows beside a pillar. They were talking, laughing, and eating. Her hands trembled slightly, and her lips quivered. She felt a stirring deep within her.

The other day Jesus had been speaking of His coming death. Peter had reprimanded the Lord, not believing the truth of His words. Perhaps none of them were aware of the truth, but she felt it deep within her soul. For some reason deeper than she could understand, she just had to do this.

She stepped forward, and instantly the laughter and voices ceased. She moved softly and directly toward Jesus, her eyes locked in His tender gaze. Those eyes that always looked as though they knew something she didn't.

She tenderly held out the beautiful flask of the costly fragrant oil of spikenard and broke the lovely alabaster. From the broken jar, the oil flowed over His head and His feet. The whole house suddenly began to smell of sweet perfume. On Jesus she lavished every bit of the expensive perfume, which had cost every cent she had earned that past year. None of the beauty would be saved for her own, personal enjoyment. Lavishing it all on Jesus was

143

far more enjoyable in her eyes than hoarding any drop for her own purposes. Even the flask itself she had broken with loving and joyful abandon. It was all for Him, every last piece. Bending down onto her knees, she took her hair, already flowing loosely about her, and wiped His feet.

She dimly heard the disciples asking, criticizing her sharply, "What waste!" "Why did she waste all of the perfume on the Lord?" "That perfume could have been used for many good causes; why is she wasting it on Jesus' head and feet?" (Matthew 26)

How could they consider this wasteful?

But then again, perhaps it was. Wasteful abandon: Extravagantly pouring oneself over Him without thought to anything else. Loving Jesus couldn't be any other way. It required *everything*…all of her time, her love, her possessions, her dreams, her beauty, her very life. But she wouldn't have it any other way. She longed to pour out her whole life for Jesus' sake. He'd given so much…He was about to give so much more, and they had no idea. He was going to die, and they were worried about wasting a year's salary?

Ah, but she was at home here. Here at his feet. There was no place on earth she would rather be, no one she would rather be with. Her heart was always at rest when she was near Him, worshiping Him, loving Him.

"Let her alone," Jesus commanded, His eyes still on Mary. "Why do you trouble her?"

Slowly He turned and looked each of His friends in the eye, with His piercing, captivating gaze. "She has done a good work for Me. For you have the poor with you always, and whenever you wish you may do them good; but Me you do not have always. She has done what she could. She has come beforehand to anoint My body for burial. Assuredly, I say to you, wherever this gospel is preached in the whole world, what this woman has done will also be told as a memorial to her." (Luke 7)

She was lovely. She would be remembered. There was something about her that would make her stand out in a crowd: A defining scent of broken, wasteful abandon. The perfume of the abandon of her life filled the entire room.

She lived a life of abandon to her King Jesus, to the Lover of her soul. The thought of another party, another hot date, keeping her hair clean and neatly styled, spending even the smallest part of her money, effort, or life on herself…these thoughts were nowhere in her mind. She was at home, in perfect rest, here at His feet. There was no place she would rather be.

The words of the sons of Korah in Psalm 83 suddenly came alive to her in that moment, as they always did when she was here with Him. "How lovely is Your tabernacle, O Lord of hosts! My soul longs, yes, even faints for the courts of the Lord; my heart and flesh cry out for the living God…For a day in Your courts is better than a thousand. I would rather be a doorkeeper [stand at the threshold] in the house of my God than dwell in the tents of wickedness."

like studying abroad

Many times our quests originate from worry about what others will think of us. What if we don't get good grades, aren't pretty enough, or don't have enough boyfriends? What will people think then? Mary found a confidence that was stronger and more influential in her life than what other people thought of her. How?

She recognized that this world was not her home. Like the heroes of the faith (see Hebrews 11), she realized that she was a foreigner passing through this world on the way to her heavenly home. Her life here on earth was short, and she wanted to be remembered for more than earthly success. She wanted a reward that would last beyond this life. She had the approval of Jesus, and that was all that mattered to her. Who cared what other people thought?

This world is like studying abroad. When I lived in Australia for four and a half months, I had an amazing time and lived every day to the fullest, but I didn't think I was an "Aussie." The entire time I was in Australia I had my passport and I knew I was an American citizen. Australia was not my end-all or be-all. It wasn't my home. I came from America and was going home to America. I was only in Australia for a short while.

Even so, I realized that I came from God (He created me) and am returning to God for eternity (when my body dies). What this world thinks of me will not matter in the long run. When I recognized that I am only here for this life and I want to make something of my life that is more than being remembered for my physical appearance, I began to see beauty in its proper perspective. My quest for beauty is only important if I am living for success in the eyes of this world. If I am living for Jesus' approval, remembering that this world is not my home, then being beautiful ultimately *just doesn't matter.*

the beauty of heaven

The beauty of heaven is completely different than the beauty of earth. Christ on the cross didn't look beautiful to us. He was broken, He was obedient. It was bloody, messy, and not attractive. But now that He has walked through that journey, now that He has borne His cross, His glory and majesty are so great we cannot begin to imagine them. His beauty is beyond our understanding while we are limited to this world and this body.

Brokenness and obedience. These are the things God chooses, the things that catch His eye. In the world, beauty is the opposite. Beauty is perfection, having it all together in every way. Sometimes we try to drag that idea of beauty into the church, and just Christianize it. But God isn't about perfection. 1 Corinthians 1-2 says God chooses the broken because then He can restore the brokenness with Himself, making the finished product more lovely than it ever could have been on its own. He chooses the obedient because they are moldable enough for Him to transform them into a work of art more beautiful than they would have been if left alone. He chooses the poor in spirit, those who know they need Him, who lean on Him, because as they walk along the journey, they become unrecognizable, covered with His glory.

It's not always an attractive journey. It's taking up our cross – bloody, messy, and not attractive. But the outcome of broken obedience is truly beautiful, truly glorious. When we are no longer seeking beauty or perfection, but only seeking and obeying Him, we come to the end of ourselves. And that, my friends, is when we come to all of Him.

Foothold #9: Find confidence by putting your eyes on Jesus, exchanging beauty for a cross.

The last step I have taken, the most recent foothold I am standing on, is this foothold of surrender. I've come full circle. My journey to freedom began with surrender and it has brought me back to a second, deeper surrender. I never could have come to this place if I hadn't taken the steps in-between, and really understood His love for me. Now in light of all He has done for me, what can I do but give my life back to Him?

If I really wanted to find complete freedom, this deeper letting go had to happen. My life had to stop revolving around me and start revolving around my Savior. When we live for ourselves, we become slaves to our quests. Freedom comes when we stop living for ourselves and start living wholeheartedly for a greater purpose. Take your eyes off of beauty and put them on Jesus. The only quest that will satisfy your heart is the quest to know Him.

Until next time,
Tiffany Dawn

Tiffany's Coffeehouse:

www.theinsatiablequestforbeauty.com

Check out the link to "11: Raspberry Chai." I have an
awesome video of my friend Kim talking about her
"mirror fast." Hear what God taught her during 30 days of
no looking in the mirror. Also check out the incredible
songs I've linked in from YouTube, and the deleted scene
titled "Eternity." Lastly, instead of a song on my CD, I've
included a recording of my song "Eternity" on the website.

July 5, 2009:

Thursday night I met with my producer, Brian Moore, and I said something about only hearing my mistakes in the (scratch) tracks...and after a pause he said, "But both the mistakes and the good parts are equally important. 'Cause without the mistakes we wouldn't have to be striving for this place...and if everything was perfect it'd be boring." I've been thinking about that – and weaknesses and such – how if everything were perfect and right, we'd never know the pleasure of experiencing beauty because we'd be accustomed to it. It's almost like without flaws you can't have beauty, without a messed up world you can't know redemption, and without our weaknesses we can't appreciate God's strength or know it at work in and through us. Really it's as if the flaws are just as integral for our understanding of what's good and right, as the good and right parts are.

Coffee Date #12:

I'm having hot chocolate - there's nothing like pure, sweet goodness to end a series of dates. What are you having?

Your Story

"This is your life.
Are you who you wanna be?"
~Switchfoot, "This Is Your Life"[1]

One book isn't going to change your life. Sometimes I hate that. It bothers me to know that when I speak somewhere, or when someone reads this book, that one, singular event is not going to radically change someone's life. That bothers me because I don't know if each person is going to take home the things they learned and make the difficult choices that are required to change a life.

But sometimes I love the fact that one book won't change a life. I love it because God has a personal, individual journey in mind for each one of us.

Everyone's journey is different. The journey to overcoming the quest for beauty takes time, gets messy, goes up and down like a rollercoaster, and is difficult, but it's *so worth it*. On the other side of the mountain there's freedom – glorious freedom unlike anything you could imagine while on the quest! Freedom to not think about food all the time, freedom to love who you are and like your reflection in the mirror, freedom to buy clothes that fit you no matter what number is on the tag of the jeans, freedom to be confident when you're single, freedom to stop focusing on beauty.

I fully believe this book can be a stepping stone to a changed life, but only if you make the choices you need to make, because a changed life comes from a day-to-day journey. I hope and pray that these coffee dates have brought insight into your life and given you some practical footholds for the journey. From here on out, what you do with these things is up to you. I'm sure this book will eventually grow dusty sitting on your shelf, but whether or not the principles you learned grow dusty is your choice.

This is your life. Who you become depends on the choices you make today and tomorrow and the day after that and a year from now. If you start on this journey, your life will be changed. But if you don't walk that journey in the hard, rubber-meets-the-road kind of everyday life, you won't be any different when you put this book down. The choice is yours.

This is your life. Are you who you want to be?[1]

beauty from brokenness

There are a few more important things you should know about my journey. When my first boyfriend and I were planning to get married, I wanted to crochet an afghan for our apartment. We went to Michael's craft store to pick out some yarn, and of course I marched straight to the babysoft, light pink rolls; but my boyfriend wouldn't have pink in his apartment, so I bought white instead.

We broke up a few weeks later and I was furious. "Not only has he ruined my life and wardrobe, but he's also ruined my blanket!" I seethed. So I marched my butt back into Michael's and bought the light pink rolls...only I didn't want to waste the effort I'd already put into finishing a quarter of the blanket in white, so I bought two other shades of pink as well. Angrily I whipped the crochet hook in and out while sitting ramrod straight in my butterfly chair.

Thoughts charged through my mind. *How dare he! Now instead of having a pink blanket, I am settling for second best. Just like in the rest of my life. I will now be forced to settle for second best in all of life because I am ruined. I've made too many mistakes.*

You can imagine my surprise when I finished the blanket and gaped at the beauty in the four shades of color. It was so much more beautiful than it would have been if I had crocheted with all light pink! I named it my "God-works-everything-for-good" blanket, because just as He turned that blanket into beauty, He's taken my mistakes and used them to bring life to others.

I didn't see this day coming. I felt hopelessly trapped in my quest. But today I am free. So free! I can breathe, I can dance, I can love. My life testifies that God can take ugly situations and turn them into beauty, taking what was meant for evil and turning it into good. I know that God has a plan for my life and for your life – and that plan is to give us a future and hope, to prosper us and not to harm us (Jeremiah 24:7). Just like God has turned my life around, He can turn your life around. You can be free. God can turn the rain into rainbows, and He can turn our brokenness into wholeness, if we'll but open up our hearts and let Him.

freedom in forgiveness

After my seminars I am often asked, "So where does this ex-boyfriend of yours live?" I just laugh the question off, but let me tell you – I've had plenty of offers to egg his car! I've also had plenty of people wonder if I am still mad at him. The answer is no.

My ex-boyfriend treated me poorly, it's true, and he was clueless of his mistakes. The annoying part was that everyone who knew him thought he could do no wrong, and all I would hear from his friends was, "Why did you break up with him? He was such a great guy! You were so lucky to have him!" How I would have loved to expose him in front of them, to let them see who he really was, the things he had said to me. *But God wanted me to forgive him.*

I was driving back to college after spring break when the Lord said, "Tiffany, you need to pray blessings on his life."

Excuse me?? My insides screamed. *What do you mean pray blessings for him?*

"Okay, God," I prayed, a little smugly, "then bless him with a lightning bolt to his head."

God was still waiting. I guess that didn't cut it.

With a deep breath I summoned all the courage I could find and started praying. "Lord, bless him with a wife whom he will think is attractive. And who will stand up to him, because I didn't." I paused. "Bless his music, but don't let people think he's perfect. Show them what he really is."

Still not enough.

"Okay, Lord, please bless him. Really bless him. Complete and fulfill all these dreams in his heart and Your plans for him." I breathed shakily. "Make him more like You. Meet him. Show him more of who You are."

The words started to pour out of me like a torrent, along with broken, dry sobs from the depths of my being. I started to really mean what I was saying. I don't know how it happened. Somehow God opened the floodgates inside me and, as I forgave him, I started to truly let go of the hurtful things he'd said. A few months later I was writing him an email, apologizing for stringing him along at the end – breaking up and getting back together only to break up again, over and over. I was apologizing to him? Yes, I never thought I would live to see that day.

The power of forgiveness.

Forgiveness is letting go of what someone did to you and not expecting anything in return. To this day, the closest thing to an apology I've received from my ex-boyfriend is, "I'm sorry I wasn't what you needed." He is still clueless about the ways he hurt me.

Before I forgave him, I was waiting for him to repent to me. I was putting my life on hold, waiting for him to realize what he had done to me so that I could have the satisfaction of seeing him broken for the things that broke me. I have since come to realize that may never happen, and I don't ever expect it to. Forgiveness doesn't wait. Instead of waiting for the other person to make amends first, or trying to hold their faults over their head (and just hurting yourself, not them), you let them go. It sounds ridiculous, but ironically it sets *you* free.

It doesn't mean forgetting. It doesn't negate the wrongs that person did to you. It doesn't mean that what you've suffered didn't matter. No, forgiveness means that you were hurt and broken by what someone else did to you (or maybe what you did to yourself) and you choose to let them (or yourself) off the hook anyway. You choose not to hold a grudge against them in your heart. It doesn't make sense in our minds and it feels as if we're losing control. The happy feelings aren't usually there at first. Forgiveness is a process. It's simply a choice we make – and continue to make – every day, every hour, sometimes every minute. It's another kind of surrender, giving up our desire to get even with someone, choosing to let them go, and eventually coming to love that person in spite of ourselves. My friend Kelly said forgiveness is like peeling an onion; layer after layer has to come off. (Oh, and it makes you cry sometimes.)

Forgiveness is one of the most powerful things we can do because it is a picture of heaven on earth. It is powerful enough to set us free and bring us further on the road of healing. Forgiveness changes *us*. We think it's only about the other person, but it's actually the next step to healing. Sometimes forgiveness also changes the life of the person we forgave. Not always, but sometimes. It's something we learn from Jesus, from the way He has forgiven all of us, who He created and yet who turned our backs on Him. Forgiveness is something I can do only by His grace and in His strength. So thank God that His grace *is* enough (2 Corinthians 12:9).

Now I can honestly say that I have forgiven my ex-boyfriend from the depths of my heart. In fact, I love him as a brother in Christ. That doesn't mean I'll ever be with him again. It doesn't mean we'll be friends. I haven't talked with him in years. But I hold no hard feelings against him in my heart. I don't think about getting even, I don't wish I could hurt him the way he hurt me, and I don't think he's a horrible person. I love him. It's a supernatural love I never could have conjured up on my own. But as I have made deliberate choices to forgive him, God has given me a supernatural love for my ex-boyfriend. He is truly forgiven.

And I am truly free. What that young man said holds no power over my life anymore. I let it go when I let him go through forgiveness. It's gone. Now I am free.

Ironically, along my journey I found everything that I originally set out for back when I started my quest. I was just thinking about that today – about how I feel beautiful, I feel confident, I feel so…*whole*. It's weird. It's different than what I imagined it would feel like. Different…but so much better. When I wanted to spend a day in someone's shoes who knew she was gorgeous, I pictured a day that was all about being admired, a day that was all about me. But the way I feel is richer. It's hard to describe.

It's the kind of beautiful that you don't even think about. You don't have to look in a mirror first. You feel so sure that you are loved and beautiful and precious, but you're not thinking about feeling beautiful. It's the kind of confidence that comes subconsciously and bleeds into everything you say or do. You're not talking yourself into feeling confident; you're just living it almost without being aware that you are. It's changed my eating habits too; instead of trying to diet, I eat when I'm hungry and stop when I'm not. There's no guilt on the occasions when I do overeat; I don't try to starve myself the next day to compensate. It's this way: I'm just not thinking about food.

What I realized today is that confidence and beauty are byproducts. They should never be our quest, because when they are our quest, they break, empty, and elude us. We will never find those things if we are searching for them.

The gospel of Matthew says to seek first the kingdom of God, and then He will add to us everything we need. It says not to worry about food or clothes or anything else, because as we seek Him, God will take care of all that (Matthew 6:25-34). All of life should be a byproduct of seeking first His kingdom.

As long as we are seeking ourselves, or our beauty, or our confidence, we will never find the fullness of what we are after. The quest will always be insatiable. But when we stop looking for those things at all, stop thinking about them entirely, and instead take up a new quest to know our Savior and give our lives unreservedly for Him, then we suddenly find a wholeness we never knew. When it's all about Him and not about what we can get from Him, there's this weird kind of confidence that comes – and it's so deep, so overflowing, so holistic.

There's no trying to fake it until you make it or tricking yourself into believing you are something you don't feel you are – it's just there. It sneaks up on you, and you don't even realize it because you're not thinking about you. But then one moment – like the moment I had today – you realize, "Something's different. Something's changed. It's like this confidence, or as if I feel beautiful, but it's more than that – so much more, because those things don't matter like they used to. It's as if I'm...*whole*."

dawn

I wish we really were sitting in a coffee shop, face to face, so I could hear your story. I wonder, as you're reading this book, what your life is like and where you are along your journey. Whatever your story is – and I do hope I get to hear it one day! – I hope that in these coffee dates we have connected. I hope that you feel like you know me, how weak I am and how strong my Jesus is.

My prayer is not that this story would change your life instantly, but that this book would be a turning point in your life. Like the dawn: an awakening of your heart to the truth, a spark to start a fire, a prod to let go of your insatiable quest for beauty and get started on your journey.

I hope that instead of feeling heavy with guilt and trying to be good enough, you have found a peaceful freedom to enjoy your new quest and journey to know the Lord, who came to give us life abundantly. "The one who calls you is faithful and He will do it" (1 Thessalonians 5:24, NIV, 1984).[2] The Lord is going to work this journey out in your life. He's not going to leave you stranded halfway through. He is able, ready, and willing to bring you all the way. He is going to complete the good work He has begun in your heart. What a comforting realization! You don't have to worry; God's got it. Just turn your heart toward Him and allow Him to walk you through your day-to-day journey. He will take you on the adventure of a lifetime and you will never be the same again.

Thank you for spending these past 12 coffee dates with me. My heart is crying as I write these closing paragraphs. I'd like to pray for you, my dear friend, as I cannot think of a better way to conclude this final coffee date.

Father, I thank You so much for the young woman who is holding this book in her hands right now. I ask that You would meet her right where she is. I thank You that as she draws near to You, You are drawing near to her, even if she can't feel it yet.

I ask that You would take her on a journey into fullness of life and freedom from the quest for beauty – that she would remember to keep an eternal perspective, and realize that her purpose in life is not to be beautiful; her purpose is to know You. As she realizes this, the rest of life will fall into its proper place.

I ask that You would reveal Your love to her – Your great and unconditional and unchanging Your love for her – and that she would never be the same again. May this be a turning point in her life, a moment in time when Your strength overwhelms all her weakness, a moment she can hold near to her heart forever, when she begins to discover the fullness of life You came to bring her.

Bless her and keep her as she journeys with You. Thank You that nothing – not even she herself – nothing can snatch her out of Your hands, and nothing can change Your love for her. And I praise You that this good work which You have begun in her life will be completed, and one day You will present her faultless before the throne of God with exceeding joy.

We love You, Lord. In Jesus' name I pray, amen.

Well, my friend, I will see you on the mountain top!

Your fellow journeyer,

Tiffany Dawn

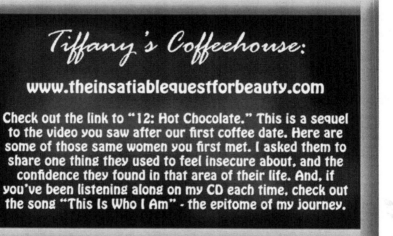

Afterward

If you do not yet know Jesus, and have never given Him your life, let me tell you – being a child of God is the most wonderful part of my life! I'm serious. If you would like to give Him your life, here is how:

The Bible says that Jesus is the way, the only way, to know God, to be set free from our sin (the ways in which we haven't pleased God), and to be saved from the punishment that sin deserves, which the Bible says is death.

God is so holy and perfect, that He cannot be where sin is. Sin deserves death – which is total separation from God, in hell, after our physical death. So God sent Jesus to take our sins onto Himself and, the Bible says, to become sin for us. Jesus died so that we don't have to spend all of eternity in hell, apart from Himself. He died because He loved us so much, and wanted us to spend eternity with Him so much, that He would stand in our place to take the punishment we deserved. It's like someone being given the death sentence, and someone else stepping in and serving the sentence for them, so that the criminal could live. It's crazy to me how much God loves us!

The central, core, and most important truth of Christianity is that Jesus came to earth, as the Son of God and yet also man, and died on the cross, receiving the punishment we deserved for our sins. He then rose from the dead and returned to heaven, just like we will find new life with God after our bodies die.

When we believe in Jesus, receive His gift of eternal life, ask His forgiveness of our sin, and give our lives to Him, then we become a child of God; we have the promise of eternal life in heaven with Him after we die; and we can know God even here in this life. Without accepting Jesus' forgiveness and believing on Him as our personal Savior, we will spend eternity in hell, and even here in this life we will not know the comfort He offers in the midst of hardship or receive His promise to work all things out for our good.

"This righteousness from God comes through faith in Jesus Christ to all who believe. There is no difference, for all have sinned and fall short of the glory of God, and are justified freely by his grace through the redemption that came by Christ Jesus. God presented him as a sacrifice of atonement, through faith in his blood..."

- Romans 3:22-25a, NIV, 1984[1]

All you have to do is ask Him. There's not a magic prayer. Just talk to Him. Ask His forgiveness for the things you have done that were not pleasing to Him, tell Him that you believe He died for your sin and was raised from the dead, and ask Him to make you His child. Then go on the journey with Him.

Reading the Bible is just one way to get to know the Lord better, as are praying and going to a Bible-believing church. It's amazing to me that God – the Creator of heaven and earth – sees us and wants to have a personal relationship with us. He already knows us so well – the Bible says that He knows the very number of hairs on our head – but He also wants us to know Him.

So there you are! I wanted to make sure you had this information in case you wanted it, so that you too can be a child of God, because from what I've found, there is no greater joy in this life than to be His. It's only in Him that we can find the ultimate satisfaction and fulfillment.

God bless you as you begin (or continue) your journey with Him.

Citations

Chapter One:

[1]Springsteen, Bruce. "Dancing in the Dark." <u>Born in the USA</u>. Sony, 1984, 1990.

[2]Dillon, Bethany. "Beautiful." <u>Bethany Dillon</u>. Sparrow, 2004.

Chapter Two:

[1]Digby, Marié. "Unfold." <u>Unfold</u>. Hollywood Records, 2008.

Chapter Three:

1. Frou, Frou. "Let Go." <u>Details</u>. Mca, 2002.

Chapter Four:

1. Orrico, Stacie. "(There's Gotta Be) More to Life." <u>Stacie Orrico</u>. Virgin Records Us, 2003.

2. *The Donut Man on Tour*, directed/performed by Rob Evans (USA: Integrity Music), VHS.

3. C.S. Lewis, *Mere Christianity* (New York: Macmillan Publishing Co., Inc., 1952), 183.

Chapter Five:

1. ZOEGirl. "Unbroken." <u>Different Kind of Free</u>. Sparrow, 2006.

2. Sheri Rose Shepherd, *His Princess: Love Letters from Your King* (Colorado Springs, Colorado: Multnomah Publishers, 2004), 12-13.

3. *The Holy Bible*, New International Version, NIV, (Biblica, Inc., 1973, 1978, 1984, 2011).

4. Max Lucado, *You Are Special* (Wheaton, Illinois: Crossway Books, 1997).

5. Leslie Ludy, *Set-Apart Femininity: God's Sacred Intent for Every Young Woman* (Eugene, Oregon: Harvest House Publishers, 2008).

Chapter Six:

1. Starfield. "Shipwreck." <u>Beauty in the Broken</u>. Sparrow, 2006.

2. Katy Hutchison, "The Story of Bob" (presentation, Nazareth College of Rochester, Rochester, NY, October 29, 2009).

3. See "Eat Drink and Be Mindful" at www.eatingmindfully.com, and "The Center for Mindful Eating" at www.tcme.org.

4. Faune Taylor Smith, Randy K. Hardman, P. Scott Richards, and Lane Fischer, "Intrinsic Religiousness and Spiritual Well-being as Predictors of Treatment Outcome among Women with Eating Disorders," *Eating Disorders* 11, no. 1 (2003): 15-26. **AND** P. Scott Richards, Michael E. Berrett, Randy K. Hardman, and Dennis L. Eggett, "Comparative Efficacy of Spirituality, Cognitive, and Emotional Support Groups for Treating Eating Disorder Inpatients," *Eating Disorders* 14, no. 5 (2006): 401-415.

5. Hillsong United. "Hosanna." All of the Above. Hillsong, 2010.

Chapter Seven:

1. Jean Kilbourne, *Deadly Persuasion* (New York, NY: The Free Press, 1999), 135.

2. See "Eat Drink and Be Mindful" at www.eatingmindfully.com, and "The Center for Mindful Eating" at www.tcme.org.

Chapter Eight:

1. Andy Warhol, *The Philosophy of Andy Warhol (From A to B and Back Again)* (Orlando, Florida: Harcourt, Inc., A Harvest Book, 1975), 63.

2. "Do You Love What You See When You Look in the Mirror?" *National Organization for Women (NOW) Foundation*, © 2000-20011, http://loveyourbody.nowfoundation.org/.

3. Kate Fox, "Mirror, Mirror: A Summary of Research Findings on Body Image," *Social Issues Research Centre*, 1997, http://www.sirc.org/publik/mirror.html.

4. "Statistics: Eating Disorders and Their Precursors," *National Eating Disorders Association*, 2010, http://www.nationaleatingdisorders.org/uploads/statistics_tmp.pdf.

5. "Women of all Sizes Feel Badly about their Bodies after Seeing Models," *ScienceDaily*, 2007, http://www.sciencedaily.com/releases/2007/03/070326152704.htm.

6. "Beauty and Body Image in the Media," *Media Awareness Network*, 2009, http://www.media-awareness.ca/english/issues/stereotyping/women_and_girls/women_beauty.cfm.

7. Jean Kilbourne, *Deadly Persuasion* (New York, NY: The Free Press, 1999), 124.

8. Gordon L. Patzer, *Looks: Why They Matter More than You Ever Imagined* (New York, NY: AMACOM, 2008).

9. Gian Paolo Guaraldi, Emanuele Orlandi, Paolo Boselli, and Kathleen M. O'Donnell, "Body Image Assessed by a Video Distortion Technique: The Relationship Between Ideal and Perceived Body Image and Body Dissatisfaction," *European Eating Disorders Review 7*, no. 2 (1999): 121-128. **AND** Shelly Grabe, Janet Shibley Hyde, and Monique L. Ward, "The Role of the Media in Body Image Concerns among Women: A Meta-analysis of Experimental and Correlation Studies," *Psychological Bulletin* 134, no. 3 (2008): 460-476.

10. K. M. Kowalski, "Body Image," *Current Health 2* 29, no. 7 (2003): 6-13. **AND** Jean Kilbourne, *Deadly Persuasion* (New York, NY: The Free Press, 1999), 123.

11. Audrey D. Brashich *All Made Up: A Girl's Guide to Seeing through Celebrity Hype...and Celebrating Real Beauty* (New York: Walker & Company, 2006), 50, 74-76.

12. Jean Kilbourne, *Deadly Persuasion* (New York, NY: The Free Press, 1999), 134.

Chapter Nine:

1. Flatts, Rascal. "Fast Cars and Freedom." <u>Rascal Flatts: Greatest Hits Volume 1</u>. Lyric Street Records, 2009.

2. *Anne of Green Gables*, directed by Kevin Sullivan, (1986; USA: Sullivan, 2001), DVD.

Chapter Ten:

1. Maya Angelou, *Wouldn't Take Nothing for My Journey Now* (United States: Bantam Books, 1994), 11.

2. Art Thomas, "Dr. Maya Angelou," *Your-Inner-Voice.com*, 2010, http://www.your-inner-voice.com/mayaangelou.html.

3. Joseph I. Williams, "Mother Teresa's Style of Leadership," *Indiana State University ITE 675 Leadership in HRD*, 2003, http://itchybon1.tripod.com/hrd/id28.html.

Chapter Eleven:

1. Fraser, Brooke Fraser. "C.S. Lewis Song." <u>Albertine</u>. Wood & Bone, 2008.

2. Francis Chan, *Crazy Love: Overwhelmed by a Relentless God* (Colorado Springs, CO: David C. Cook, 2008).

3. ZOEGirl. "Good Girl." <u>Room to Breathe</u>. Sparrow, 2005.

4. André French. (2002). "In Light of You." Unpublished.

5. Paul Oakley. "It's All About You (Jesus Lover of My Soul)." <u>Because of You</u>. Survivor, 2011.

Chapter Twelve:

1. Switchfoot. "This Is Your Life." <u>The Beautiful Letdown</u>. Sony, 2004.

2. *The Holy Bible*, New International Version, NIV, (Biblica, Inc., 1973, 1978, 1984, 2011).

Afterward:

1. *The Holy Bible*, New International Version, NIV, (Biblica, Inc., 1973, 1978, 1984, 2011).

About the Author

A 2004 entry in Tiffany Dawn's diary reads, "I would do pretty much anything to be beautiful." Her teenage years in the suburbs of Albany, NY, were spent homeschooling and pursuing her interests, including music and journalism. Like so many other American youths, Tiffany eventually became immersed in ads and social pressure to be fashionable, attractive, and land the perfect relationship. It's a mindset that can control people from teen years into adulthood, but Tiffany found freedom and confidence in Jesus Christ.

Today, 25-year-old Tiffany is sharing her battle for self-esteem through a seminar she developed called "The Insatiable Quest for Beauty,"™ a blend of music, storytelling and preaching that delivers an authentic, personal message to male and female listeners. Tiffany also hosts "coffee dates" online (www.theinsatiablequestforbeauty.com) and released her first full-length album, "This Is Who I Am," in 2011. Tiffany received a BA in music from Roberts Wesleyan College (2007) and her MS in music therapy from Nazareth College (2012), both in Rochester, NY.

Tiffany admits she has bad hair days and is currently single. She's not-so-secretly in love with crocheting, pretzels, marshmallows and long walks. Find her on Twitter: @quest4beauty, visit www.tiffany-dawn.net, or send an email to tiffany.dawn.iqb@gmail.com.

- Bio by Leah Stacy

The CD:

"This Is Who I Am"

You can order Tiffany's CD
on iTunes or Amazon.

Made in the USA
Middletown, DE
27 June 2015